MW01399823

The Conversion of Armenia to the Christian Faith

W. St. Clair-Tisdall

About Pyrrhus Press

Pyrrhus Press specializes in bringing books long out of date back to life, allowing today's readers access to yesterday's treasures.

W. St. Clair-Tisdall's *The Conversion of Armenia to the Christian Faith* looks at the process that brought about the crucial religious changes in the modern country. From the preface:

"DURING the last few years the world has witnessed a terrible spectacle. We have seen a Christian nation in Asia, of the same Âryan blood as ourselves, suffering the most cruel wrongs at the hands of the Turks and their confederates, the Kurds. We have seen members of this Christian nation, men and women and little children, massacred in tens of thousands, and our illustrated papers have presented us with photographic views of some of these terrible scenes. We have read of large numbers dying a martyr's death rather than embrace Islâm, and have heard of those who had less courage and faith being driven at the point of the sword to repeat the creed of the Arabian Antichrist. We have beheld something more strange still — the Christian nations of Europe hampered in their endeavours to put a stop to this state of things by their mutual distrust and jealousy of one another. And thus, as we draw near the end of the nineteenth century, our newspapers are quietly discussing the question whether or not Turkey will succeed in exterminating the whole Christian population of her Armenian provinces, or in forcing upon them, at the sword's point, an apostasy worse than death.

It may not be amiss, therefore, at the present juncture to inquire into the early history of the Armenian nation, and more particularly to study the conversion of Armenia to the Christian faith. The writer of the following pages began this investigation for his own information, and is impelled to offer to the public the result of his studies in this field of research, partly by the interest attaching to the subject itself, and partly by the hope of thereby doing something to enable European Christians more readily to sympathize with their Armenian brethren in their present affliction.

My residence in Julfâ, the Armenian suburb (if I may so style it) of Isfahân, and the fact that I had for a time the superintendence of an Armenian congregation here in connexion with the Church Missionary Society, have not only given me an opportunity of studying the Armenian language, but have even rendered such a course of study incumbent upon me. I have thus been enabled to draw my information at first hand from Armenian historians, some of whom were contemporary with many of the most prominent actors in the great work of converting Armenia to faith in Christ. This has more than compensated for my not being able to refer to any European works whatever on the subject, except in so far as a limited classical library and a few patristic works could render me assistance. This little work is therefore based entirely upon original Armenian authorities, as far as its main argument is concerned."

PREFACE

DURING the last few years the world has witnessed a terrible spectacle. We have seen a Christian nation in Asia, of the same Âryan blood as ourselves, suffering the most cruel wrongs at the hands of the Turks and their confederates, the Kurds. We have seen members of this Christian nation, men and women and little children, massacred in tens of thousands, and our illustrated papers have presented us with photographic views of some of these terrible scenes. We have read of large numbers dying a martyr's death rather than embrace Islâm, and have heard of those who had less courage and faith being driven at the point of the sword to repeat the creed of the Arabian Antichrist. We have beheld something more strange still – the Christian nations of Europe hampered in their endeavours to put a stop to this state of things by their mutual distrust and jealousy of one another. And thus, as we draw near the end of the nineteenth century, our newspapers are quietly discussing the question whether or not Turkey will succeed in exterminating the whole Christian population of her Armenian provinces, or in forcing upon them, at the sword's point, an apostasy worse than death.

It may not be amiss, therefore, at the present juncture to inquire into the early history of the Armenian nation, and more particularly to study the conversion of Armenia to the Christian faith. The writer of the following pages began this investigation for his own information, and is impelled to offer to the public the result of his studies in this field of research, partly by the interest attaching to the subject itself, and partly by the hope of thereby doing something to enable European Christians more readily to sympathize with their Armenian brethren in their present affliction.

My residence in Julfâ, the Armenian suburb (if I may so style it) of Isfahân, and the fact that I had for a time the superintendence of an Armenian congregation here in connexion with the Church Missionary Society, have not only given me an opportunity of studying the Armenian language, but have even rendered such a course of study incumbent upon me. I have thus been enabled to draw my information at first hand from Armenian historians, some of whom were contemporary with many of the most prominent actors in the great work of converting Armenia to faith in Christ. This has more than compensated for my not being able to refer to any European works whatever on the subject, except in so far as a limited classical library and a few patristic works could render me assistance. This little work is therefore based entirely upon original Armenian authorities, as far as its main argument is concerned. The chief Armenian authors whom I have consulted are those mentioned in the following list :–

Armenian Authorities.

	Author and name of work quoted.	*Century when composed.*	*Edition used.*
I.	Agathangelos, *Patmonthiun* .	IV	Tiflis, 1882.
2.	Faustus Byzantiuus, *Patmonthiun Hayots*	IV	St. Petersburg, 1883.
3.	Moses of Khorenê, *Patmonthiun Hayots* or *Azgabanouthiun Tohmin Habethean*	V	Amsterdam, 1692.
4.	Koriun, *Sb. Mesrovpah Keankhn* .	V	Venice, 1854.
5.	Elisha (Eghishê), *Vasn Vardanats ev Hayots Paterazmin*	V	Venice, 1864. Tiflis, 1879.
6.	Eznik Koghbatsi, *Eghds Aghandots*	V	Constantinople, 1873.
7.	Thomas Ardsrounî, *Patmonthiun Tann*	X	St. Petersburg, 1887.
8.	Chhamchheants, *Patmonthiun Hayots,*	XVIII	Venice, 1784-86.
9.	Khrakhçhan, *Hamarot Patmouthiun*	XIX	
10.	Sylvester Hovhannêsean, *Hamarot Patmouthiun Hayots*	XIX	Julfâ, 1877.
11.	*Haikakan Hin Dprouthian Patmonthiun*	XIX	Venice, 1886.
12.	*Haikakan Thargmanouthiunkh* Nakhneats	XIX	Venice, 1889.
13.	Stephen Palasanean, *Patmonthiun Hayots, skzbits minchhev mer Ôrerě* .	XIX	Tiflis, 1890.

Besides these I have made use of extracts from Lazarus Pharpetsi (fifth century), Zenobius (fourth century), and other early writers, quoted at some length in Chhamchheants and *Haikakan Hin Dprouthiun* ; and I have found most valuable the selections from a variety of modern writers (mostly Armenian, but some Russian) contained in *Ĕntiṛ Ḥatouadsneṛ* (Tiflis, 1889).

The system of transliteration I have used for Armenian names (except the best known, e. g. Tigranês) is an exact one, but it would weary the ordinary reader and be unnecessary to the Armenian scholar to explain it at length. Suffice it to say that the *a* is always long, and is pronounced like the German *a* in *aber,* while the dotted *ṛ* and the *d* are cerebral letters, and a parasitic *y* is heard before *e* and a *v* before *o*. *Kh* printed in italics is pronounced like the German *ch,* and *kh* not so printed is sounded as in *inkhorn.*

Besides the Armenian writers mentioned above, I also owe something to Eusebius, and less to other early Greek and Roman patristic writers. I have of course consulted Herodotus, Xenophon, and Polybius, Livy, Tacitus, Suetonius, Velleius Paterculus, &α, for that portion of the work in which aid could be expected from them. Any other writers to whom I am at all indebted I have mentioned in the footnotes *in loco.* For *dates* I have generally depended upon Stephen Palasanean's able and valuable work mentioned above.

It may be asked why I have continued the narrative up to the fall of the Arsacide dynasty in Armenia, instead of pausing at the death of Gregory the Illuminator. The answer is that the Armenians themselves, in the days of which I have written, rightly considered that Gregory's great work remained incomplete until the translation of the Bible into Armenian was finished in A. D. 436, as we learn from Lazarus Pharpetsi, a contemporary historian. I trust the interest of the subject-matter of the narrative will serve to plead my excuse for taking the same view.

In conclusion I have only to express my hope that the manifold defects and shortcomings of this little volume—written during the few hours at night which I could spare from my missionary duties—will be pardoned, and will not be suffered to hinder its usefulness. I may be permitted to add that I agree generally with the views expressed, and still more with the hopes implied, in reference to his nation's future destiny in the following passage from an Armenian writer of the present century :

'From all indications it appears that this very nation has been by Divine Providence chosen as the means of spreading Christianity and civilization in the East. There is no doubt that the circumstance that this Christian population is diffused over a great extent of country—from Morocco to China—and at the same time that all its members are bound to one another by religious ties, has a great historical and universal significance.'

W.St.Clair-Tisdall
Julfâ, Iṣfahân, Persia.

CHAPTER I

THE COUNTRY AND ITS PEOPLE

> . . . ' Nec Armeniis in oris,
> Amice Valgi, stat glacies iners
> Menses per omnes.'
> Horace, *Carminum* ii. ix. 4-6.

Armenia is a land of extremes. Owing to its geographical situation, and the great variety to be found in the configuration of the country, at different seasons and in different parts of the land, the most tropical heat and a cold that is almost Arctic may be met with. It, however, has also regions where the climate may well be compared with that of the Azores and the islands that lie off Spain and Italy. This great variety of climate is in large measure due to a corresponding variety in the elevation of the land. Many of the highest mountain-peaks of Europe are lower than the great plateaus from which flow the silver streams which ultimately develop into such rivers as the Euphrates, the Tigris, the Kouṛ, the Araxes and the Aṛadzan. The Simplon and St. Gothard Passes are lower than the blue surface of beautiful Lake Sevan, round which – till lately—there were clustered thousands of populous villages. On the other hand, some portions of Armenia are actually below the level of the ocean, as is the case with the shores of the Caspian Sea, the surface of which is eighty-three feet below that of the Mediterranean.

In the district now known as Diârbekr, where stood the renowned ancient city of Tigranocerta (Tigṛanakert), it is said that sometimes in summer the heat of the sun is so excessive that it actually melts the leaden waterspouts of the houses. In other parts of the country the surface of the ground is for six months in the year completely covered with snow, and the temperature falls to 26° Réaumur below zero. Caravans compelled to travel in such weather have to cut their way with axe and saw and spade through the ice and snow, and are fortunate if they escape being buried by an avalanche or lost in a snow-storm. Ancient Armenian writers tell us that King Sanatṛouk, when an infant, was buried in the snow for three days, and then found alive resting on his nurse's bosom. His grandson, Tiṛan, is reported to have been killed by an avalanche after a reign of twenty years. Strabo tells us that, under such circumstances, the buried traveller's only chance of escape lay in forcing up through the superincumbent mass of snow his alpenstock, in the hope that, before too late, it might lead to his being discovered and disinterred from his living tomb. In the times of the Arsacide kings, special officers were appointed, whose duty it was to keep the passes open, and to provide in suitable places rest-houses for the use of travellers. St. Chrysostom, who during his last exile experienced its severity, speaks of an ' Armenian winter ' as proverbial, which indeed the united testimony of Greek and Byzantine travellers, historians and poets from Xenophon's time onwards shows to be no more than the truth.

The rivers and smaller streams which flow down from the higher table-lands have, during thousands of years, eaten their way deep into the earth, and are in many cases to be found flowing between precipitous banks hundreds of feet high. The deep shadows cast by such banks upon the distant surface of the swiftly-flowing stream beneath make the water seem black ; and hence is explained the frequent title of ' Black Water ' given in our own time to many of these rivers. In ancient times the art of irrigation was carefully studied, and the abundant water-supply rendered the country extremely productive. Its naturally fertile plains and rich meadow lands early invited the indus-trious population of Armenia to engage in pastoral and agricultural pursuits, and large herds of cattle were reared. The religion of the people during Arsacide times was not very different from the Zoroastrianism of Persia, and we may well believe that, like that religious system, it encouraged agriculture and every form of husbandry. Armenia is probably the native land of the vine and the rose, and Columella calls the apricot the *Malum Armeniacum,* or Armenian apple, for a similar reason. Wheat, barley, rice and other cereals seem to have been cultivated from the earliest times in Armenia, and ancient writers mention its mules, buffaloes, sheep, goats, asses and cattle as being most numerous. Xenophon praises Armenian horses, and says that, though somewhat smaller than the Persian, they were both sturdy and spirited. The Bible tells us that ' they of the house of Togarmah ' (i.e. the Armenians, who still often call themselves by this name) traded in the marts of Tyre with war-horses, ordinary horses and mules. The country is also very rich in minerals, and its mines were in ancient times carefully worked. The north-western districts produced salt and beryl ; Aghtsnikh and Touṛouberan had copper, iron and lead mines; in the districts of Aiṛaṛat and Speṛ gold was found ; in Phaitakaṛan cotton grew ; Touṛouberan was famous for its honey and manna ; Goghthn produced abundance of grapes, from which great quantities of a sweet-scented kind of wine were made. The district of Taikh provided figs, pomegranates, quinces, almonds ; that of Outi was rich in its olive-trees. Cochineal was produced in Aiṛaṛat. On the banks of the river Araxes and in the regions of Siunikh and Phaitakaṛan grew forests of valuable timber of many different kinds, which were largely used in other lands for building palaces.

The richness of Armenia in all kinds of minerals, the fertility of its soil and the abundance of its varied products naturally tended to incline the minds of its inhabitants towards trade and commerce. Hence we find that in the most ancient times they were famed as traders, a talent which still distinguishes them in whatever part of the world they are found. The position of the country in almost the centre of the ancient world, and the fact that its large rivers gave its people access to three important seas, still further favoured the development and extension of its commerce. The river Pison or *Chorokh* unites it with the Black Sea, the Araxes *(Eṛaskh* with the Caspian, the Euphrates and Tigris with the Persian Gulf and the Indian Ocean. In part of its course too the Euphrates approaches the Mediterranean, in the neighbourhood of Samosata and Marash. In this way Armenia was enabled to enter into commercial relations with almost every portion of the world as known to the ancients. Doubtless trade was first carried on by land, but, when maritime commerce advanced, that by land gradually declined. Armenian merchants, following the course of the Kouṛ and Araxes to the east, and availing themselves of the commercial routes afforded by the Caspian Sea and the rivers Jaxartes and Oxus, sent their wares to Bactria, Sogdiana, Parthia and India. By way of the Euxine and Mediterranean they found their way to Greece and Italy, and also to Cappadocia and Phoenicia. They figured in the marts of Tarsus and (as we have seen) of Tyre, and dealt in gold, silver, precious stones, valuable cloth fabrics, dyes, oil, honey, and other articles of merchandise. They kept up constant intercourse with Nineveh and Babylon during the days of their glory, whither, following the course of those two great natural highways the Tigris and Euphrates, they exported wine, fruit, timber and many other of the products of their country, importing in return carpets, silks and the most valued luxuries of wealthy Mesopotamia and even of distant India. Herodotus gives a most interesting account of their skin boats, fastened to a wooden frame, not altogether unlike the coracles of the ancient Britons, in which the Armenians of his own day descended the Euphrates, bringing large jars of wine and other products of their country for sale to Babylon.

The greater part of Armenia is between 8,000 and 3,000 feet above sea-level. It slopes gradually towards the Euphrates, the Kouṛ, the Caspian Sea, and the plains of Armenia Minor. The mountain generally known as the Greater Ararat, but more correctly styled Mount Masis, is over 17,000 feet high. The Lesser Ararat or Lesser Masis and Mount Aṛagds have an altitude of 13,000 feet. To the south-west of Mount Ararat are Mounts Bouṛdogh, Soukavêt and Seṛmantz, which form portions of the northern branch of the Taurus Range. Other important peaks are Mounts Sasni, Gṛgour, Endzakhiaṛs and Aṛtos. Towards the south are the Gordyaean Mountains or the Mountains of Kurdistân, upon one of the peaks of which general Eastern tradition says that the Ark rested.

The country abounds in rivers and streams of all varieties of size and importance. The three largest and most important are the Euphrates, the Tigris and the Araxes, the latter celebrated for its swiftness and violent floods, alluded to by Virgil in the verse *Pontem indignatus Araxes*. This latter stream plays a most important part in

Armenian history, and one of the saddest incidents connected with it is that, when Shâh 'Abbâs, King of Persia, who lived in the time of Queen Elizabeth, was carrying away a large body of unfortunate families from Armenia to found the present town of New Julfâ near Isfahân, vast numbers of the wretched captives—some accounts say as many as 10,000—perished in attempting to cross the Araxes. Their descendants still show manuscript copies of the New Testament and service books stained with the water of that stream on that sad day. The Euphrates rises in the Kaṛni high-lands, waters Upper Armenia, and forms the boundary between Armenia Major and Armenia Minor. On the right bank it receives the Gail (Lycus), and on the left the Aṛadsan (also styled the Armenian Euphrates), which rises in the Bagṛevan Mountains. The sources of the Tigris are two —one of its branches rising not far from the southern bank of Lake Dsovkh (below Khaṛbeṛd), the other at the village of Oloṛ in the province of Ḥashtenikh. The two branches meet near Akl and form the Tigris. The Araxes receives several tributaries and ultimately joins the Kouṛ in the desert of Moughan, and falls into the Caspian Sea. Among the many lakes of Armenia three are of special importance. These are Lake Sevan or Gegham, Lake Van or Bznovnikh and Lake Uṛmi (Urumiah) or Kapoutan. In ancient times Armenia was considered to consist of two parts, Armenia Major (the part of the country which alone originally bore the name of Armenia) and Armenia Minor. Armenia Major varied in extent, at different epochs, but when at its greatest extent its boundaries were—on the north, Egeria, Georgia and Alvania (Albania), from which countries it was divided by the Moskhikean Mountains and the river Kouṛ (Cyrus) ; on the east by the Caspian Sea, Persia and Media ; on the south by Assyria and Mesopotamia ; on the west by Asia Minor, from which it was divided by the Euphrates during part of its course.

According to the old division of the country, Armenia Major consisted of fifteen provinces and 189 cantons. The central province of Ararat was the original home of the Armenian people, and generally claimed authority over the whole country. To the east of this lay the provinces of Siunikh, Aṛtsakh, Outi and Phaiṭakaran ; to the north, Gougaria and Taikh ; to the west, Upper Armenia and Armenia Quarta or Dsophkh ; to the south, Touṛoubeṛan, Vaspouṛakan, Mokkh, Aghtznikh, Koṛchaikh and Persian Armenia. Armenia Minor extended from the Euphrates to the river Halys, and was divided into three provinces, called by Latin geographers Armenia Prima, Armenia Secunda and Armenia Tertia.

Any student of Armenian history will be struck with the very great influence which in all ages the physical conformation of the country has exercised upon the nation's destiny. The large and small mountain chains which abound throughout the country cut it up into a large number of small districts very difficult of access from neighbouring districts of Armenia, though often easily accessible from the side on which they face foreign countries. The inhabitants of the valleys and small plains, of which the habitable parts of Armenia are in large measure composed, are often separated from one another, as by almost insuperable barriers, by the intervening mountains or the almost impassable rivers and mountain torrents which occur in such large numbers throughout the land. Hence, from the most ancient times of which we have any knowledge, the country was divided up into a large number of petty states, often hostile to one another, and not unfrequently claiming a complete or semi-independence. The kings of the central district of Ararat claimed to hold sway over the whole country, and constantly made attempts to exercise it, but they rarely succeeded— never for very long—in subduing all these small communities and in attaching them in loyal obedience to the crown. Having therefore continually to contend both with external foes and with internal disunion, the latter being especially active when enemies were threatening the kingdom from without, the sovereigns were unable to consolidate the monarchy and extend the king's authority to the extreme limits of the country. The door was therefore always left open to the incursions of the neighbouring nations. Add to this the want of any strong natural boundaries which might serve—like the Alps do in the case of Italy—as a barrier against the assault of the enemy, the natural feeling of the people, which inclined them in a very special degree to make every man a law unto himself and to refuse obedience to any superior, and we can well understand why it was that during historical times Armenia has rarely for any length of time been free, united and autonomous.

The country has by turns been subject to the Egyptians, the Babylonians, the Assyrians, the Persians, the Macedonians, the Romans, the Parthians, the Byzantine empire, the Sâsânian Kings of Persia, the Arabs, the Turks, the Mughals, and is now divided between three empires, the Turkish, the Persian and the Russian. It is a moot point among those best acquainted with the physical features of the country whether it would ever, under any conceivable circumstances, be possible for Armenia to be formed into one strong, united and independent monarchy. But it may be urged on the other hand that, were the Armenians united, like the Swiss, in the resolute determination to secure the independence of their country, no degree of physical difficulty in maintaining constant intercommunication between the various parts of this Switzerland of Asia would hinder Armenia, when once set free, from maintaining her freedom against all comers.

The glimpses which we are enabled to obtain of the civil life and habits of the ancient Armenians are interesting if somewhat scanty. Herodotus, Xenophon, Quinctius Curtius, Strabo and other classical writers, when supplemented by native authors of later times, enable us to form some idea of the government, the customs and the degree of civilization which existed in Armenia in early times. The first form of government seems to have been patriarchal, as was natural among a simple-minded, peaceful, industrious population largely engaged in agricultural and pastoral pursuits. Aram, the sixth in succession from the mythical Ḥaik, the ancestor of the nation, is said to have been the first to assume the title of king and to endeavour to assert his authority over all the tribes that inhabited Armenia. When the Assyrian empire was at its height, and claimed to exercise sway over the south-western part of the country, its rule was carried on by means of native Armenian chiefs, subdued by force of arms, whose principal obligation was to collect the tribute imposed on them by the conqueror.

From the time of Tigranês 1 (who ascended the throne in B. C. 565), it seems that civil and political institutions among the Armenians began to take more definite shape. The impulse which Tigranês gave to his people exerted an influence not only on the government, commerce and trade of the country, but also on the conditions of family life. Under that king the first signs of opulence become visible, and we find a distinction growing up between ' city ' and ' country ' people and ' villagers.' An attempt seems also to have been made to reduce the language to writing by using Greek and Zend letters—just as at an earlier date the Vannic syllabary of the cuneiform inscriptions found near that lake was borrowed from that of Assyria.

During the celebrated Retreat of the Ten Thousand, Xenophon passed through a portion of Armenia. His description of the terrible cold, the immense masses of snow, the great sufferings of his troops on the march, enables us perhaps to realize something of the miseries which at the present moment so many of the unfortunate Christian fugitives of Armenia are enduring amid their inhospitable mountains. But, besides this, he gives us a graphic description of the domestic life and social condition of the people in his time, and thus enables us to see what these must have been for many centuries previously. Each village or town had its own local chief or mayor, who ruled in accordance with unwritten ancestral laws and customs. The dwellings of the people were similar to those still found in some parts of the country and in Georgia. They were in large measure subterranean, the roof, however, rising high above the ground. The doors leading to these habitations were narrow and deep, and looked at first sight like the opening of a well, but widened out within. These doors were in general opened only for the ingress and egress of the lower animals, for the human inhabitants entered their dwellings by means of a ladder leading to a small opening in the roof. The house within presented something resembling the 'happy family' of an Irish peasant of the present day. On one side of the hut were stalls, fastened to which (in winter, when Xenophon visited the country) were sheep, goats and cows, while domestic fowls shared their shelter and food. On the other side were ranged receptacles for stores, full of wheat, barley and other kinds of grain, and also large jars filled with beer, which Xenophon describes as ' a kind of wine made from barley, which pleases those who are accustomed to it.' In some villages they had old and sweet-smelling wine. The method employed in order to drink the beer was rather peculiar. In the jars stood jointless hollow reeds of different lengths. When required, these were inserted in the liquor, to enable the consumer to drink it purified of the grains that floated on its surface. The people had various kinds of oil, with which they anointed themselves as the Greeks did with the olive oil of Attica. They set before their somewhat unwelcome guests an abundant variety of food, consisting of lamb, kid, pork, fowls, wheaten and barley bread, wine and beer.

We have thus in this introductory chapter shown something of the nature of the country and the character of the people with whom our narrative deals. We have endeavoured to lift a corner of the veil of antiquity which shuts out from our sight much that is interesting regarding the scene upon which the *dramatis personae* whom history introduces to our notice were called upon to act out their little part in the tragedy of human existence. We have learnt something of the country which the Armenians, wherever they are scattered throughout the world, still lovingly call their Fatherland. In the next chapter we purpose to deal briefly with the main facts of their history up to the time of Christ, for whose advent in the fullness of time they—like all other nations of the world—were, though unconsciously, being prepared.

We cannot conclude these preliminary remarks more suitably than with the words of a Russian writer, who had deeply studied the history and character of the Armenian people. 'From the point of view of the struggle for existence also,' he[1] says, 'the permanence and continued duration of that small nation causes us to wonder, since for centuries it has remained like a wedge driven in between other great peoples. Mighty Assyria and Babylon, the dread despotism of the Persian empire, the sway of the Parthians, the Macedonians, the Romans, the Arabs, have come to an end. Very great nations have perished and vanished from the face of the earth ; but the Armenian nation has not only continued to exist, but moreover, full of hope and of vitality, is now burning with a thirst for knowledge and a love for exertion. It still plans to cast off the yoke it has borne for a thousand years ; it continues to improve its language, to cultivate the sciences, and to press forward, and has already made no little progress in these respects. . . . A nation which has been able to preserve its individuality from the days of Nimrod and Semiramis up to our own times, and also in some measure to maintain its own distinctive type, its customs, its language and its religion—and that too notwithstanding the fact that no nation, not even excepting the Hebrew, has been called upon to endure such sufferings—must never be forgotten in history.'

CHAPTER II

EARLY HISTORY TO THE TIME OF CHRIST

'Ελευθεριας ἐπεθύμουν' καλόν γάρ μοι δοκεῖ εἶναί και αὐτου ελευθερου εἶναί, καί παισίν ἐ λευθερίαν καταλιπεῖν

The Armenians trace their descent from a legendary hero Ḥaik, son of Thorgom or Togarmah, son of Gomer, son of Japheth. Their early and celebrated historian, Moses of *Khoṛenê,* even ventures to give a personal description of the great ancestor of his nation. He was, we are assured, ' a well-built hero, with curly locks, tall, strong-armed and sweet-looking, a skilful archer, possessed of a good memory, prudent and brave.' Leaving Babylon shortly after the Confusion of Tongues, Haik, with three hundred of his descendants and a large number of adherents, retreated to the mountains of Armenia, and there established his people under his own patriarchal government. The tyrant Bel, by some identified with Nimrod, who had compelled the people of Shinar to worship him as a god, sent messengers to command Ḥaik to return to Babylon and submit to him. On his refusal, Bel marched against him with a countless host of warriors, who like storm-clouds covered the face of the land. Ḥaik's followers were few but brave. The rival hosts met in battle on the shores of Lake Van. The battle lasted for days, and was fiercely contested ; but at last dauntless heroism prevailed against overwhelming numbers. Bel was defeated with terrible loss, and fled from the field with the remnants of his army. Ḥaik pursued him and slew the tyrant with a well-aimed arrow. He caused the giant's body to be embalmed, and carried it to a district called Ḥarkh, where he buried it on the top of a hill, that the tyrant's tomb might to all generations preserve the memory of his defeat and record the bravery and prowess of his conqueror.

Ḥaik then turned his attention to the welfare of his subjects. He reduced the aborigines under his mild but firm sway, built cities, and established law and order throughout the land. During his lifetime Noah died, and was buried on the top of Mount Niphatês. Noah's wife, Noemzaṛa, was interred in the province of Maṛand. The Armenians assert that their tongue is the oldest in the world, being that spoken by Noah and retained in the country where he and his descendants dwelt when they emerged from the Ark and settled in the province of Ararat.

The Armenian language is an Âryan tongue, not remotely connected with Sanskrit, Greek and Latin, though more closely akin to ancient Persian, the language of the Zend Avesta. To the present day many words found in that ancient tongue and in the cuneiform inscriptions of Darius, though lost in modern Persian, may be heard from the lips of an Armenian peasant. Its affinity to the Keltic languages, spoken by the Cymru and other descendants of Gomer, is in many respects striking. This, though not in itself a sufficient test of an ethnic relation between the Kelts and the Armenians, strengthens the proof afforded by the character of the people that they are indeed children of Gomer and one of the most ancient of the nations of the world. From time immemorial also they have dwelt in the fertile though mountainous country which the Bible asserts to have been the cradle of the human race after the Deluge. Nor do recent scientific investigations, pointing as they do, according to general (though not universal) belief, to the conclusion that the ancestors of Âryans, Semites and Turanians once dwelt together in some lofty Asiatic region, tend in any degree to refute this assertion.

Those who have any personal acquaintance with the Armenians are struck by the great resemblance in character which still exists between them and their Irish and Welsh kindred. There is the same sanguine temperament with its quickly changing alternations of joy and sorrow, of hope and despair, the same independence of character and ardent love of liberty, the same burning patriotism, the same long-lived memory of past wrongs and unquenchable longing for revenge. The description which classical writers give us of the ancient Gauls, of their impetuous and all but resistless valour in the charge, of their readiness to lose heart and break, like billows against a rock, when unsuccessful in the assault, exactly describes the Armenians whose deeds in their frequent contests with the Roman and the Parthian armies are recorded in the pages of ancient history. The apparent fickleness of the Irish character too, the tendency to quarrel among themselves and to split into numberless parties unless when under the absolute control of a master-mind to whom all are compelled to yield unhesitating obedience, even to the death, has been in all past ages, as it is even to the present day, the distinguishing feature and the bane of the Armenian race. Prone to superstition, credulous of the marvellous, proud of the ancestral glory of his nation, and tenacious through all vicissitudes of the religion he professes, the Armenian in his good qualities as well as in his bad is the Kelt of the Asiatic continent. Hospitable, generous and mean, prudent and rash, a keen trader and unscrupulous bargainer, industrious, capable of the greatest fidelity and the utmost depths of treachery, the Armenian character has in it much worthy of praise and much else deserving of reproach. But alike in its good and in its bad qualities it presents clearly marked characteristics ; and, though down-trodden for ages by Egyptian and Assyrian, Persian and Parthian, Macedonian and Roman, and last of all by Mongol and Turkish conquerors and oppressors, the type and the race to which it belongs show, as has already been said, a marvellous vitality, and give promise of continuance until the end.

Armenian history as recorded by native chroniclers is so largely fabulous that we must, for the record of almost all that occurred previous to the establishment of the Arsacide dynasty in B.C. 150, depend solely upon the scattered notices that occur in the recently deciphered inscriptions of Egypt and Assyria, and on the narrative of Greek and Roman historians. From the cuneiform inscriptions at Van and elsewhere deciphered by Professor Sayce, we learn that a more ancient race inhabited at least those parts of the country before they were taken possession of by the Armenians themselves. But as early as the Eighteenth Dynasty, in the seventeenth century before Christ, the name of the Armenen or Remenen occurs on the Egyptian monuments, and we are informed that they dwelt in the mountainous regions to the north of Mesopotamia. Thothmes III, one of the greatest of Egyptian conquerors, in the annals of his wars engraved on the walls of the temple at Karnak, records the exploits of his warriors in Armenia, as well as in Syria, Mesopotamia and the adjacent regions. During the concluding years of his reign, the Armenians were subdued and compelled to pay him tribute. Seti I and Raamses II also warred with them. When Assyria succeeded to

Egypt in the sovereignty of Asia, her kings also made frequent incursions into the same regions. Asshur-nazir-pal, Shalmaneser II, Tiglath-Pileser II, Sargon and Sennacherib boast of the massacres they perpetrated in Armenia and of the spoils they brought home thence. Armenia was tributary in after years to the Medes, but revolted under King Tigranês I, who is said to have been an ally of Cyrus the Great. In Darius' time, Armenia formed a portion of the thirteenth nome of the Persian empire, and Herodotus[1] informs us that this nome paid a tribute of 400 talents yearly to the imperial treasury. An Armenian and Phrygian contingent marched in Xerxes army on his invasion of Greece, and was led by Artokhmês, who had married a daughter of Darius. Herodotus describes the soldiers of both these countries as fully armed and wearing armour. On the fall of the Persian empire, Armenia passed under the yoke of the Macedonian conqueror, and became somewhat later a portion of the territory of the Seleucides. Its rulers had then long lost the royal title, but reassumed it when, under Antiochus Epiphanês, offers of assistance from Rome encouraged them to rebel and endeavour to shake off the yoke of the Syrian monarch. The troubles that ensued led the Armenian nobles to invoke the assistance of the newly-created Parthian monarchy. Arsacês, a brave Parthian had in b.c. 238 succeeded in shaking off the authority of the Seleucides and in establishing himself as King of Parthia. His fifth successor, Arsacês VI, readily accepted the invitation of the Armenians, and marching with a large army into the country, defeated and expelled the Seleucide garrisons, and appointed his own brother Valarsacês (Vaghaṛshak) King of Armenia (b. c. 149). The Arsacide dynasty in that country lasted for centuries, and under it the Armenians enjoyed a greater measure of prosperity than ever before or since.

The Parthian empire, of which Armenia thus became a part, included Parthia, Media, Persia, Elam, Meso-potamia, and, it is said, a portion of Syria and the Panjâb as far as the river Indus. The various portions of this vast territory were—as had been the case in all previous great Oriental empires—very imperfectly welded together, and remained in most instances under the government of their own kings, who paid tribute and rendered homage to the ' King of Kings,' as the Parthian sovereigns, in imitation of the ancient Kings of Persia, styled themselves. As the Armenians (if we may accept the statement of their own historians) had not been subdued by the Parthians, but had voluntarily yielded to them and invited them to take possession of the country, they were treated with particular favour. Vaghaṛshak was given by Arsacês VI the 'right of the second throne,' that is, he was recognized as ranking in the empire next after Arsacês himself. To him was assigned the duty of guarding the western frontier of the empire against the attacks of the Seleucides, the only formidable adversaries whom the Parthians had at that time to fear, the name and fame of Rome having as yet hardly reached their ears. Armenia thus became a 'buffer state,' to use a modern expression, and in consequence after some centuries again became what she had been in some measure in the past—the battle-field upon which the various rival candidates for the empire of the East strove for supremacy. But for some considerable time after the establishment of the Arsacide dynasty in Armenia the country possessed sufficient unity and strength to preserve it from this cruel fate.

The reign of Vaghaṛshak is of peculiar interest in Armenian history, on account of the great advances in civilization and order which the country made in his time and under his guidance and encouragement. He did not become ruler of the whole country without a struggle. Morphylicês, ruler of Cappadocia, who claimed the sovereignty of Armenia in virtue of his descent from the royal family that had last reigned there, gaining support from some of the nobles, advanced into Armenia to dispute the throne. Vaghaṛshak met him near Colonia in Armenia Minor. A fearful contest took place with great loss on both sides, but it ended in the total defeat of Morphylicês and his death on the field of battle. Vaghaṛshak then became supreme throughout the whole country, and gradually extended his kingdom until it embraced a very large part of Asia Minor and reached in the north to the Caucasus Mountains. Resolved to be the real and not only the nominal monarch, Vaghaṛshak removed the capital to Nisibis, on the borders of the territories of Syria, and began to summon to court the greater nobles, who had hitherto resided on their own estates and preserved a kind of semi-independence of the sovereign. By conferring on them new titles and creating new offices about the court, he succeeded in retaining them for the future in large measure about the person of the sovereign, and in thus preventing them from acquiring power and influence in various parts of the kingdom, which might result (as it had done in the past) in dividing the country against itself. The king introduced a new departure by appointing deserving persons to be nobles, without giving them fiefs and feudal tenure of large tracts of land, in accordance with the old order of things, Vaghaṛshak fixed the right of succession to the throne in favour of the eldest son of the monarch, and provided that all other sons should be sent away from court and assigned princely residences in another part of the kingdom. He introduced many other excellent military and political regulations, put the country into a complete state of defence, and made many wise laws, not a few of which he borrowed from the Parthians (who in their turn were indebted for them to the more civilized nations they had subdued), but some were derived from the ancient customs of the country.

The king's inquiry into these ancient customs and regulations aroused his interest in the history of the nation over which he was called to rule. He had found the whole of the country in a state of confusion and disorder, the very services in the temples not being exempt from sharing in the general disorganization. There existed no historical records of any importance, from which he could gain information regarding the past. Vaghaṛshak accordingly resolved to enlist in his researches the aid of his brother the King of Parthia. He therefore sent to his court a Syrian, learned in Greek and other languages, Mar Ibas Katina by name, with a letter requesting permission for him to search the royal archives for the requisite information. The letter itself, as given by Moses of Khoṛenê, is an interesting document, and, if genuine, throws some light upon the social and political position of Armenia at the time. It runs as follows :—

'Aṛshak, king of land and sea, whose person and image are verily as those of our gods, and his good fortune and destiny superior to those of all kings, and the vastness of his intellect as far above theirs as the heavens are higher than the earth !—Vagharṣhak, thy younger brother and ally, who has by thee been appointed King of Armenia, [prays thus] :—" Mayest thou be prospered with all success."

' Whereas I received from thee a command to take thought for virtue and wisdom, I have never been regardless of thy counsel, but on the contrary have provided for and pondered everything as far as my mind and intellect sufficed. And now, having through thy providence established my kingdom, I have resolved to ascertain what persons have ruled Armenia before me, and whence originated the various orders of nobility that exist here. For it is not evident that there were any fixed orders here, or any orders of service in the temples, nor is it clear who is the first and who the last in rank of the chiefs of this country, nor is anything else orderly, but everything is confused and wild.

' Wherefore I beseech thy Majesty to command that thy royal library be opened to the person *who* has come to thy august Majesty, in order that, having discovered that which is desired by thy brother and son, he may carefully bring the exact truth, and that I may know of a surety that my desire (which is of my own free will) is in accordance with thy pleasure. Mayest thou be prosperous through thy glorious dwelling amid the gods ! '

In accordance with this request, Arsacês sent Mar Ibas Katina to Nineveh —so the story runs—with permission to search the royal archives there for information about Armenia. Mar Ibas is asserted to have found there a Greek translation of the history of Assyria, made by the orders of Alexander of Macedon, and to have compiled from it the history of Armenia from the earliest times. This history was still extant in the time of Moses of Khoṛenê (a. d. 400), and from it he derived the fabulous accounts of early kings and heroes that have up to the present time passed among Armenians as authentic history.

Under Vagharṣhak, in agreement with the rule made by Arsacês when he appointed him king, Ar-menia was independent of Parthia except in two respects: (1) Arsacês reserved to himself alone the right of coining money for the use of the whole empire ; and (2) Arsacês as King of Kings was recognized as the *first,* and the King of Armenia as *second,* in the empire.

Vagharṣhak was succeeded in b.c. 127 by his son Aṛshak, and he in turn by Aṛtashês I, his son (b.c. 114). Aṛtashês was a warlike and ambitious prince. His soldiers are said by Armenian poets to have been so numerous, that when they all discharged their arrows together the sun was darkened, and when every one of them threw down a single stone in one place a mountain was formed! This king defeated Mithridates II, King of Parthia, and forced him to resign in his favour the proud title of King of Kings, and to content himself with ranking second to Aṛtashês. The latter struck money in his own name, and planned to accomplish what Xerxes had failed to do—achieve the conquest of Greece, which was then subject to the Romans. With this object in view he formed an alliance with Mithridates Eupatôr (Mithridates VI), King of Pontus, to whom he gave in marriage his daughter Aṛtashamah and rule over the shores of the Caspian and Black Seas.

Aṛtashês carefully trained his son Tigranês in all warlike exercises, hoping that he would succeed him and carry all his ambitious schemes to a successful termination. Building a large fleet on the Black Sea, Aṛtashês crossed over from Thrace to Boeotia and caused great alarm in Greece. The Romans being then engaged in a life or death struggle (the Social War, B. c. 90-89), could not meet him in the field, but bribed his generals to murder him. 'Alas for my fleeting glory ! ' he cried with his latest breath.

Tigranês II succeeded his father Aṛtashês in B.C. 89, having for two years previously been associated with him in the government with the title of King of the Province of Ararat. Under this monarch, Armenia reached the acmé of her power and military glory, which, however, faded very soon, and left her exhausted and a prey to foreign conquerors. Inheriting the title of King of Kings, Tigranês, in alliance with Mithridates VI of Pontus (his sister's husband, according to Armenian historians, his father-in-law, as Roman writers say), extended his sway until at one period he ruled over Armenia, Media, Arabia, Atropatenê, Mesopotamia, and Syria. Plutarch says that he forced dethroned kings to wait on him as his servants, and that four such unfortunates attended him to hold his stirrups and assist him when he mounted his horse. Our limits do not permit us to dwell upon the three fierce wars between the Romans and Mithridates, in which Tigranês became involved as ally and relative of the King of Pontus. When in B.c. 71 Lucullus defeated Mithridates and captured his fortress of Cabeira, the latter monarch took refuge with Tigranês, whom Velleius Paterculus and other Roman historians call ' the greatest and most powerful king of his own time.' Tigranês refused to surrender the fugitive to the Romans. Lucullus thereupon entered Armenia and captured Tigranocerta, styled by the Romans the capital of the country. In B.C. 68 Lucullus defeated Tigranês on the banks of the Arsanias, and would have captured Artaxata (Aṛtashat), the second chief town of Armenia, but for a mutiny among his troops, which compelled him to withdraw into Mygdonia. He then advanced against Nisibis (called by Armenian writers the capital city of Armenia at the time) and captured it. In a war with Orodês, King of Parthia, Tigranês was compelled to surrender to the latter the title of King of Kings. On the other hand, the Armenians claim that their troops took part with the Parthians in the great defeat inflicted on the Romans under Crassus, 30 miles north of Charrae (Haran), in B.C. 53. An Armenian general, Baṛzaphṛan, in command of an army of Armenians and Parthians, entered Syria in B.C. 51, and advanced as far as Jerusalem, which he captured, though it fell into the hands of the Romans once more under Ventidius Bassus in B. C. 39. Tigranês died after a reign of fifty-three years, and was succeeded by his son Aṛtavazd I. This king abandoned himself to gluttony and luxury, and was captured by Antony in B.C. 36, who, binding him in golden chains, sent him prisoner to Cleopatra at Alexandria, where he was beheaded. Antony then took possession of the whole of Armenia, and made Alexander, his son by Cleopatra, king.

Antony's defeat and death in his war with Octavian soon enabled the Armenians to shake off the Roman yoke, at least in the southern part of the country. The northern long remained subject to them, having Artaxata (Aṛtashat) as its capital. Classical and Armenian historians seem hopelessly at variance about the history of Armenia at this period ; but it appears clear that Armenia proper falls for a time out of the ken of Armenian writers, who style the Kings of Osroênê (whose capital was Nisibis, and afterwards Edessa) Kings of Armenia. Aṛsham, son of Tigranês, became king of this part of the country about B.C. 28, and reigned until B.C. 3 or 5, when he was succeeded by his son Abgar. In the reign of this king our Lord Jesus Christ was born ; and, shortly after His Ascension, it is said that Christianity was first introduced into Armenia. The details of this great event, however, we must reserve for a later chapter.

CHAPTER III

MYTHOLOGY OF THE ANCIENT ARMENIANS

'Ο θεός ὁ ποίησας τον κόσμον και πάντα τάευ αὐτῷ . . . ἐποίησέν τε εξ ἑνός παν ἔθνος ἀνθρώπων κατοικεῖν ἐπι παντός προσώπου της γης . . . ζητεῖν τον θεου, εἰ ἄρα γε ψηλαφήσειαν αυτόν καί εὕροιεν.—Acts xvii. 24-27.

While the various tribes which composed the Armenian nation doubtless had each their own favourite deities, many of which had a purely local importance, it may be observed as a general truth that the ancient religion of Armenia, though at one time greatly influenced by Assyrian mythology, was very similar to that of the ancient Persians as preserved for us in the Zend Avesta. Comparison between the Rig-Veda of India, the Zend Avesta of Persia, the Homeric Poems and Hesiod's Theogony of Greece, and the mythology of the Romans, the Teutons, the ancient Scandinavians and the Norse tribes, shows that, under different names, very much the same deities were worshipped in ancient times by all the nations of the Âryan race. But the chief deities of Armenia, in their names as well as in their attributes, certainly show a very strong Îrânic influence ; which, however, had more power to change the names of the deities than to make any very real alteration in the attributes ascribed to them.

The chief god of the Armenian mythology was styled Aṛamazd, the same name as that of the Ahura Mazdâ of the Zend Avesta and of the inscriptions of Darius and Xerxes. But while Ahura Mazdâ seems to have had no consort and no children, Aṛamazd was considered as the father of at least all the more important of the Armenian deities. He was the ' Creator of Heaven and Earth,' and was omniscient, the giver of all earthly good things, the bestower of health and wealth, of fullness and abundance. His most common title was ' Aṛi Aṛamazd, ' Aṛamazd the brave, the noble. He, like the other deities, was invisible, and was in the most ancient times worshipped like the rest without the use of any image or similitude. But when Armenia was brought into contact with Greek art and civilization, the effect was felt in a great increase of idols. Many of the Arsacide monarchs favoured the introduction of Greek methods of worship. Tigranês II was especially zealous in this respect. He is said to have erected in many parts of the country images of the Greek deities, which his father had brought from Greece itself. In each case, however, these were identified with the Armenian gods and goddesses of somewhat similar attributes", in accordance with the general custom of ancient heathenism. Thus the image of Zeus was erected in Aṛamazd's temples, and considered as representing Aṛamazd himself. The place especially dedicated to the worship of Aṛamazd was the renowned ancient fortress of Ani, near the present town of Gamakh, in the canton of Daṛanaghikh in Upper Armenia, where the Arsacide kings were usually buried. The worship of Aṛamazd, like that of Ahura Mazdâ in Persia and Varuna in India, gradually fell more and more into the background, and was supplanted by that offered to more popular deities, who appealed more to the affections and imagination of the people. Aṛamazd's consort, regarded as co-existent with himself, was named Spandaṛamet. She typified the fertility of the ground, and was invisible, but her visible symbol was the earth itself. She corresponds therefore to the Greek Dêmêtêr or Mother Earth, the Speñta Ârmaiti or ' Holy Wisdom ' of the Zend Avesta.

One of the most popular and most generally worshipped of the Armenian deities was the goddess Anaḥit, daughter of Aṛamazd, who corresponds closely with the Greek Artemis. She was entitled the ' Mother of all sobriety and self-respect, the benefactress of the whole human race, she through whom this land of Armenia exists and flourishes, the glory of our nation and its vivifier.' The Kings of Armenia entreated her to be the guardian of their country. In many places temples were reared in her honour, and the treasures of the state were often deposited in them to be under her charge, and were thus dedicated to her. Her most important and perhaps most ancient temple was at the town of Eṛiza, near the modern Eṛznka : a second was at Aṛtashat, in the province of Ararat : a third and very famous sanctuary was at Ashtishat, on the river Aṛadzan, at the foot of Mount Khaṛkhê, in the province of Taṛôn (near the present St. Kaṛapet). Her image was also worshipped in Vaspouṛakan. These images were often of precious materials, and she was called by a variety of titles, such as ' Golden Mother,' ' Gold-bearer,' ' Goddess of the Golden Image,' &c. Her importance in ancient mythology is also evidenced by the survival of her titles in the form of modern proper names of men and women, e.g. *Voskan, Voskeḥat,* or, in a shortened form, *Ôskô,* all meaning *golden.* Even when Christianity was introduced and became the established religion of the country, her worship was continued, though concealed under that of the Virgin Mary. Anahit, the old Persian Anâḥita, means ' the spotless,' ' the undefiled one.' This idea seems to have long been retained in Armenia, though in Persia she seems all too soon to have been identified with the Assyrio-Babylonian Beltis, the Mylitta of Herodotus, who was regarded as the goddess of generation and practically of impurity. In this respect her history is similar to that of the Greek Aphroditê and the Roman Venus, whose identification in later times with the Oriental Nature-goddess led to unspeakable degradation of an originally high and noble conception.

Next to Anaḥit in popularity and importance was her sister Astghik (= Asteria, the ' Starry Goddess'). Originally the goddess of the planet Venus, the star of the evening and of dawn, she was also worshipped as the goddess of beauty. She was the wife of the deified hero Vaḥagn. In the time of the Arsacides there stood in the province of Taṛôn a temple sacred to Astghik, which was, however, generally called 'Vaḥagn's noom,' as her consort was associated with her in worship. The influence of her worship is still felt in proper names of women, popular names among Armenian females being still Aṛouseak (the Bride) and Lousaber (Light-bringer), names of the same planet Venus.

Another sister of Anaḥit and daughter of Aṛamazd was the goddess Nanê. Through similarity of names she has been identified with the Babylonian deity Nana. The name is doubtless the same, and it means *mother* or *grandmother* in Accadian and Turkish as well as in Armenian. As a deity named Baṛsham is said to have been introduced into Armenia from Syria, the same may perhaps be true of Nanê, but we can hardly regard this as proved. Nanê was the goddess of wisdom, or, more strictly speaking, of cleverness and ingenuity, characteristic still of Armenian women, of whose most admired qualities Nanê may be said to be the deification and the impersonation. Tigranês II erected an image of Athênê in the town of Thil, and it was worshipped as that of Nanê, it being thought proper to identify the Armenian with the Greek goddess of wisdom.

Next in order comes the god Mihr, identical with the Avestic Mithra, from the headdress of whose priests some of our bishops have borrowed their *mitres,* both name and thing ! The word *mithra* signified a ' friend.' He was regarded as son of Aṛamazd and brother of Anahit, Astghik, and Nanê. Miḥṛ, like Mithra, was the invisible witness to and guardian of covenants and agreements, and the punisher of covenant-breakers and of all who did not keep their promises and carry out the agreements they had made. His visible symbol was the sun in the sky, and on earth the sacred fire. Both of these were from very ancient times worshipped in Armenia. But instead of the perpetual fire maintained in Magian shrines as the emblem of Mithra, only once a year was a pyre kindled in Miḥṛ's temples in Armenia as the symbol of the god. The chief sanctuary of Mihr was at the town of Bagayaṛichn, in the province of Deṛjan in Upper Armenia, where it is said that Tigranês II erected in his honour an image of Hêphaistos, which he had brought from Greece. The great popularity of the god Mihr is proved by the frequency of the occurrence of his name as an element in masculine proper names, e.g. Miḥṛdat (Mithridates), Miḥṛnaṛseḥ, &c. The old Armenian month Miḥṛakan or Meḥekan was named from the god. The sun itself was worshipped as a male deity, often under the name of Mihr, while the moon was adored under the title of ' Fire Sister.' The stars were also honoured as deities. The worship of the sun made a very lasting impression upon the mind of the people, and long after the establishment of Christianity in Armenia there existed a sect styled Aṛevoṛdikh, or ' Sons of the Sun.' These for a long time continued to exist in spite of many attempts to suppress them. The month of Aṛeg (= sun) and the province of Aṛevinkh ('partisans of the sun '), near the river Araxes, are additional signs of the popularity of this deity. It is said that an ancient name of the city of Van was Shâḥ-Miḥṛ-Keṛt, or ' city of the sun-king,' but the first of the three component parts of this name is *Persian,* not *Armenian.* The city of Vostan near Van was dedicated to the moon. Associated with the worship of the heavenly bodies was that of water, the tutelary genius of which was entitled ' Fountain Brother.' *Light* itself was regarded as an emblem of the sun-god ; hence the Armenians, like the Persians, early adopted the habit of worshipping with their faces turned towards the east—another old heathen custom still approved by some Christians in other lands also.

Another of the principal deities of ancient Armenia was Vaḥagn, who has been identified with Hercules. Some authorities state that he was originally a mortal King of Armenia, who died about B.C. 520, and that after his death he was deified. This reminds us of Euhêmerus' theory regarding the Greek deities, which early Christian writers in general knew how to make good use of. Whether true or not in the present instance, it is hard to say. As a god, Vaḥagn was said to have been born in a supernatural manner, having sprung into being amid the labour-pains of heaven, earth and the Red Sea. Vaḥagn gathered out all ' dragon-like buckthorns ' from the soil of Armenia, and delivered the nation from the influence and tyranny of evil beings. His strength and courage were boundless, and won for him the favour, and ultimately the hand, of the beauteous Astghik herself. Armenians early began to approve of the sentiment expressed in the words ' none but the brave deserves the fair ' : and even to the present time, in some of their villages, a young man is deemed unworthy of a wife until he has succeeded in forcibly carrying her off from her father's house. Vaḥagn's temple was styled Vaḥeyanean ; and many precious gifts, including vessels of gold and silver, were there offered to him. He and his consort Astghik were also considered as *luminaries* as well as guardian deities. It is related of Vaḥagn that he stole the straw of the deity Baṛsham, and carried it off to his own temple. The galaxy is formed of bits of the straw which he dropped on the way home. In Armenian it is therefore called not only 'the milky track'

[Kathnadzir] but also 'the way of the straw-thief ' or 'of the medicine-stealer ' *(Haṛdgoghi* or *Daṛmanagoghi chanapaṛhn).* The likeness of this tale to one told in Grecian and Vedic mythology is worthy of note. One of Vahagn's titles was ' Vahagn, who plays with dragons.'

Among secondary deities, the principal and the most popular was Amenabegh, the ' All-fruitful,' who was the tutelary genius of fruit-trees and of the vine. He rewarded the vine-dresser for his toil by giving him an abundant crop of grapes. Amenabegh may therefore be compared with the Bacchus of classical mythology. He was very extensively honoured in Armenia, and prayers were offered to him to guard and protect the fruit from the sudden and violent showers of rain, and from the hail-storms and violent tempests which are so common in mountainous countries like Armenia. The special seat of his worship was Bagavan, 'town of the god.' A great annual festival in honour of Amenabegh was held there from the first to the sixth day of the month of Navasaṛd (August), the first month of the ancient Armenian year, when the fruit was generally ripe, or nearly so. Great multitudes used to attend this festival, at which the first fruits of the produce of the trees were offered to the god, horse-races were held in his honour, and an antelope was let run or a dove set free, that all might know that Amenabegh was the giver of nourishment and joy to man and beast and bird alike. One of the titles of this deity was *Amanoṛ,* ' renewer of the year,' because of the fact that the year opened with his festival. The fact that Armenia was probably the original home of the vine, and the great resemblance between the attributes and festivals of Amenabegh and those of Bacchus, render it more than probable that the two deities are identical, and that his worship was introduced into Greece from Armenia.

Besides Amenabegh, who was one of the goddess Spandaṛamet's assistants in promoting the fertility of the ground, of which she was the tutelary deity, there were a number of other minor deities, the names and attributes of many of whom are unknown to us. But Hoṛot and Moṛot, the heroes of Mount Masis (Ararat), are of interest because, though apparently connected with the *Maruts* of Hindû mythology, and hence originally wind-gods (their appellations, as we find them in Armenian, have been altered so as to make them seem to be derived from the Armenian words for 'father' and 'mother' respectively—in the genitive *hoṛ* and *moṛ),* their names, under the forms Hârût and Mârût, have been received into the Qur'ân, and hence into Muhammadan tradition and mythology, as those of two fallen angels.

We must not, however, forget to mention, among the gods of secondary rank, the deity Tiṛ or Tiuṛ, also worshipped by the ancient Persians. He was Aṛamazd's scribe, and it was his duty to keep watch over men's actions, and to enter all their deeds, both good and bad, in a volume called ' The Book of Life.' The common people entitled him ' the writer god ' ; but by the priests he was styled ' the pen of Aṛamazd and teacher of the arts.' After men's death, Tiuṛ took their spirits to the presence of Aṛamazd, who judged them, and awarded rewards or punishments according to the record of their deeds as contained in ' The Book of Life.' Old women in Armenia still curse their enemies by uttering the words, ' May the writer (i.e. Tiuṛ) carry you off!' Other phrases which have survived from heathen times are, ' *Tiṛ ôn andṛ* ' and ' *Tiṛ ôn i bats taṛ,'* ' God forbid ! ' (lit. 'Tiṛ, avaunt ! Tiṛ, carry it away ! ') The word *tiṛatsou,* which at one time meant *learned, skilful, a diviner,* but now means *lecturer, clerk, chorister,* also survives to bear witness to Tiṛ's reputation as the sender and interpreter of dreams, and the teacher of the sciences. He was said to have written men's fate on their foreheads ere their birth ; and the expression ' It was written on my forehead' is heard among the Armenians as well as among the Hindus to the present day. Tiṛ seems to have resembled Hermês also in being the messenger of the gods, and thus a kind of mediator between them and their priests, to whom he conveyed the warnings and directions sent them by Aṛamazd and the other deities of the first rank. Tiṛ's chief sanctuary was at the town of Eṛazmoin, between Eṛevan and Aṛtashat. Other deities of less importance were those known as the Haṛlêzkh, the Khajkh ('brave ones'), Parik ('the good,' cf. old Persian Pairaka, the modern *Perî),* Houshkaparik, Hambeṛou, &c. These purely Armenian names, preserved in Christian literature, belonged to beings which probably resembled the Greek tutelary deities of fountains, trees and mountains. Some suppose that these indigenous deities were worshipped in more ancient times, and yielded to the incursion of Assyrian first and, later, of Persian gods. The Vannic inscriptions mention among the gods *Haldia,* goddess (?) of the moon, *Pamis* (heaven), and *Diaspas* (the sun). But these probably belonged to a different race altogether, the language of these inscriptions having more relation to Georgian than to Armenian.

Certain superstitious ideas that still linger among the Armenian peasantry confirm what has already been said regarding the very great resemblance that existed between their ancient heathenism and that of Persia. The Zoroastrians believed that the parings of one's nails must be carefully preserved from the danger of being found by the *daèvas* or demons, ministers of Aṅrô Mainyus or Ahriman, who would otherwise make darts out of them, to the injury of mankind. To the present day the Armenian peasant tells his children that it is a sin to let the parings of one's nails fall on the ground, or to throw away the trimmings of one's hair. When a tooth has fallen out, it should be taken to a church or some other sacred place, and there concealed in a chink in a wall or pillar. Every Armenian has, as his attendant and guardian, a good or a bad spirit, who accompanies him from the cradle to the grave.

But though the likeness between Armenian and Persian heathenism was great, one great difference must be noticed. No trace of the Persian dualism, of the existence of Ahriman, the Evil Principle, coexistent with Ahura Mazdâ, the Good Principle, can be found in Armenian mythology. The evil spirits were called *devs*—the Persian *daèvas*—but they do not seem to have had a recognized chief. Good spirits were called *Hṛeshtaks,* the same word as the Persian *Ferishteh* (or *Ferver).* The place of punishment after death was styled *Dzhokhkh,* the modern Persian *Dûzakh.* These words are still retained in the language, but with a Christian meaning.

In the earliest times worship and sacrifices were usually offered in the dim and mystic shades of the great forests, which then spread over the greater part of the country. Images, altars and temples, if existent at all were few in number, as among the ancient Germans in the time of Tacitus. The introduction of these accessories of worship into the southern and western provinces of Armenia was due to the influence of neighbouring nations. Sacrifices used long to be offered to the sun on the tops of the mountains, and to the moon, especially on the summit of Mount Sepouḥ. The heads of families and chiefs of tribes were also, in ancient times, entrusted with the duty of acting as priests. Ḥaik's son and successor, Aṛmenak, is said to have planted the Sônean forest, from the gentle or violent rustling of the leaves of which omens used to be taken. After Vaḥagn's deification and the accession of the Arsacide monarchs, the civil and the religious headship of the nation became separate from one another, the latter remaining as the inheritance of Vaḥagn's sons and their descendants. The ancient religious capital of the country was the city of Aṛmavir, which was originally the political capital also, but continued to be recognized as the chief seat of worship long after other cities had supplanted it in respect to its civil position. Vagharshak built a temple there and erected images in honour of the sun and moon .

CHAPTER IV

FIRST INTRODUCTION OF THE GOSPEL

Οὕτω δητα οὐρανίω δυνάμεi και συνεργίᾳ, ἀθρόως οἶά τiς ηλίου βολη, την σύμπασαν οἰκουμίνην ὁ σωτήριος κατηύγαζε λόγος—Eusebius, *Eccl. Hist.* ii. 3.

At the time of our Lord's birth, Armenia was divided into two separate portions, called respectively Great and Little Armenia. The latter district extended from the Gordyaean Mountains to the Eu-phrates, and had as its capital the Greek city of Nisibis. Greek art and civilization had long exercised a great influence upon the whole of Syria and Mesopotamia ; but the Roman and Greek writers seem to regard the kingdom of Osroênê, as that of Armenia Minor was generally styled, as in large measure Syrian. As is well known, the Roman government claimed the suzerainty over Mesopotamia ; and Aṛsham, who died King of Osroênê in b. c. 3, and left his title to his son Abgar, was in reality little else than their deputy, holding his position, like Herod the Great in Palestine, only by the favour of his imperial master.

Abgar, being devoted to the service of the heathen gods, refused to permit the image of Augustus to be erected in the temples of his dominions. Herod Antipas, learning this, laid a charge against him before the emperor, and accused him of disloyalty. Finding that all his efforts to clear himself were in vain, and offended at the treatment accorded at Rome to the ambassadors he had sent to plead his cause, Abgar determined to revolt from the Roman yoke, and to cast in his lot with the kindred family who then held the throne of Persia. With this object in view, he removed the seat of rule from Nisibis to Edessa, and began to strongly fortify the latter city. Moses of Khoṛenê tells us that the king carried with him to his new capital the images of the gods whom he worshipped and the religious archives stored up in the temples at Nisibis. Just when Abgar thought everything was ripe for rebellion; relying on the assistance of the Parthians, Aṛshaviṛ, the Parthian king, died, and left his kingdom a prey to confusion and civil war. Abgar felt himself called upon to restore order, and accordingly marched into Persia and put an end to the strife which had there broken out between the rival claimants to the vacant throne (a. d. 21). This expedition, through God's good providence, was overruled to the conversion of Abgar, and to the opening up of both Armenia and Persia to the light of the Gospel. The story is told by Eusebius and by the ancient Armenian historian, Moses of *Khoṛenê,* who profess to have learnt it from the archives of the kingdom of Osroênê, written in Syriac .

On his expedition to Persia, Abgar was struck with a very severe illness, which some Armenian writers tell us was leprosy, and which all the skill of his court physicians was powerless to heal. While in vain endeavouring to find some means of relief, he learnt that the Roman emperor Tiberius had been informed of his intended rebellion, and, believing that Abgar's expedition into Persia had been undertaken mainly with the hope of entering into an alliance with that empire, was about to inflict on him condign punishment. In order to avert this, Abgar in the first place entered into an alliance with Aretas, King of Arabia Nabataea, whose daughter Herod Antipas had divorced, and sent a body of Armenian troops to aid Aretas in his war against Herod. Herod's army was defeated with great slaughter ; but the Romans, hearing of the trouble brewing in Armenia, Mesopotamia and Syria, sent Marinus to Caesarea as governor, with a large army, with orders to restore order. Hearing of this, Abgar sent three Armenian nobles of high rank to Marinus at Caesarea, together with a copy of the treaty he had made with Aṛtashês, the new King of Persia, that the Romans might understand that he was loyal in his allegiance to the emperor, and had no intention of rebelling. The ambassadors were received with great honour by Marinus at Eleutheropolis, and succeeded in their efforts to prevent a breach between the emperor and King Abgar. But their visit to Palestine had another and a far more important result, for there they heard the fame of Jesus of Nazareth, whose miracles of healing were then attracting great attention. Of some of these they were enabled to become eye-witnesses themselves. On their return to Armenia, these nobles, remembering that their sovereign had completely failed to obtain healing by ordinary means,

informed him of the miraculous power and the Messianic claims of Jesus.
The whole Eastern world was, as Suetonius informs us, at that time full of expectation that a great ruler would soon appear in Judaea and establish his dominion over the whole world. The coincidence between the Messianic prophecies and hopes of the Jews on the one hand, and the strange and only slightly less clear traditions of the advent of a great Deliverer preserved in the Zend Avesta of Persia and the Sibylline books of ancient Rome and represented to us by Virgil's glorious Fourth Eclogue on the other, had doubtless turned towards Jerusalem the eyes of pious and truth-seeking men everywhere. The visit of the Persian Magi to the Infant at Bethlehem is only one indication of the extent of this expectant longing. It is not at all unlikely, therefore, that Abgar, on hearing the report of his messengers, was greatly stirred. At last the long-expected Prince had appeared ; and not only so, but was actually healing in Galilee and Judaea those afflicted with diseases which no human skill could cure. Abgar's bodily affliction naturally made him the more anxious to benefit at least by the healing power of our Saviour, and the news which his messengers brought him left no doubt of His willingness and ability to grant his request.
Abgar therefore wrote a letter to Christ, and sent it to Him to Jerusalem by the hands of his courier Ananias. Later Armenian accounts state that Ananias was also accompanied by an able portrait-painter, who had received orders from the king to request permission to paint Christ's picture and bring it back with him to Edessa to Abgar, in case the Saviour Himself declined to accede to the king's written request that He would come and heal him of his illness. The king also directed his messengers to offer sacrifices to the True God in His Temple at Jerusalem.
They reached the Holy City on the very day of Christ's triumphal entry into Jerusalem, and endeavoured to approach Him in order to present the king's letter to Him. Not being able to do so, however, they gave it to Philip, and asked him to deliver it and to procure them an audience. This, we are told, is the meaning of the incident recorded in the twelfth chapter of St. John's Gospel (vv. 20-34), where certain 'Greeks' (*Ἕλληνες),* who had come up to worship at the Feast of the Passover, were presented to our Lord. Christ saw in them the representatives of the heathen world, then longingly looking for someone to give them the light of life, and prophesied that
His crucifixion would draw all men unto Him (ver. 32). The Armenian tradition that these ' Greeks ' were Abgar's messengers has nothing directly contrary to it in the use of the word Ἕλληνες in the original, since this word is often used in the New Testament to denote any who were not Jews. The tradition is at least as old as Moses of Khoṛenê (died a.d. 487), who mentions it as an undisputed fact *(Patm. Ḥayots, Ḥat.* ii. kl. 29), and was probably believed long before then, for in the ancient Armenian version of the New Testament made by Mesṛob (died a.d. 441) the word Ἕλληνες in this passage is translated merely 'heathens.'
Eusebius, and after him Moses of Khoṛenê, gives a version of the letter which Abgar is said to have addressed to Christ on this occasion, and which Eusebius tells us was still preserved in his own time in the library at Edessa. Although all modern critics rightly regard this letter and our Lord's supposed reply to it as undoubtedly spurious, it may be of interest to enter them both here, in order to complete the narrative. Abgar's letter ran as follows :—
'Abgar, Toparch of Edessa, to Jesus the good Saviour, who has appeared in Jerusalem, greeting.
" I have heard of Thee and Thy cures, which are being performed by Thee without drugs and medicines. For, as report says, Thou dost cause the blind to recover sight, the lame to walk, and Thou cleansest lepers, and drivest out unclean spirits and demons, and healest those tormented with long-continued sickness, and raisest the dead. And having heard all these things about Thee, I decided in my mind on one of two conclusions—either that Thou art God, and having come down from heaven Thou doest these things—or that, doing these things, Thou art the Son of God. Therefore I now write and entreat of Thee to take the trouble to come to me, and to heal the disease which I have. For indeed I hear that the Jews are murmuring against Thee and wish to do Thee violence. I have a very small and noble city, which will suffice for us both.'
When our Lord had read this letter and saw Abgar's faith in Him, He directed Thomas to write a reply to it from His own dictation in the following terms :—
' Blessed art thou, who hast believed in Me without having seen Me. For it is written concerning Me that those who have seen Me will not believe Me, and that those who have not seen Me shall themselves believe and live. But whereas thou didst write to Me to come to thee, it is necessary that I should here accomplish all those things for which I was sent, and that, after having accomplished them, I should then be taken up to Him who sent Me. And when I am taken up, I shall send unto thee a certain one of My disciples, that he may heal thy sickness and give life to thee and to those that are with thee.'
Having received this letter, Abgar's messengers entreated permission to paint a portrait of Christ, in accordance with their master's orders. The required permission was accorded them, but the painter's hand failed to perform its task in delineating Christ's divine features. Seeing this, the Saviour took a towel and, applying it to His countenance, impressed upon it a marvellously correct picture of Himself, and sent it to Abgar with the letter above quoted, intending thereby to relieve his sufferings and strengthen his faith. Abgar, on reading the letter and receiving the portrait, worshipped the latter, and took courage, looking hopefully for the fulfillment of Christ's promise to send him a teacher to instruct and heal him.
This story as here related bears distinct marks of a later age, and it has received much embellishment from later Armenian writers which is not to be met with in Moses of Khoṛenê or in Eusebius. The story of the portrait and of the worship paid to it by Abgar could not have originated until the worship of pictures had been introduced into the Church. The letters ascribed to Abgar and to Christ bear evident marks of a clumsy forgery. The account of the

interview which Abgar's messengers had with our Lord is possibly but not probably true. On the other hand, it seems rash to reject the whole narrative (as many writers do) as fabulous. It may perhaps be better to hold that a certain substratum or residuum of fact underlies the tale. It is certainly neither impossible nor improbable, taking into consideration all the circumstances of the case, that the fame of our Lord's miracles of healing may have reached Edessa, and that Abgar's illness may have led him to look longingly for the arrival in his country of a disciple of Christ able to heal him. This would prepare the way for a favourable reception being given to the earliest preachers of the Gospel on their arrival in Mesopotamia and Osroênê, which must have taken place soon after the Ascension.

'After that Jesus was received up,' says the old Syriac document quoted by Eusebius, ' Judas (who is also called Thomas) sent unto him (Abgar) as an apostle Thaddaeus, one of the seventy. He coming dwelt with Tobias the son of Tobias. And when news was heard concerning him, it was told to Abgar, saying, " An apostle of Jesus has come hither, according as He wrote unto thee." Thaddaeus accordingly began in the power of God to heal every sickness and every disease, so that all men did marvel. But when Abgar heard of the mighty and wonderful works which he did, and how he healed, he suspected that this was he of whom Jesus had written, saying, " When I am taken up, I shall send unto thee a certain one of My disciples, who shall heal thy sickness." Having therefore called for Tobias, with whom he abode, he said, " I have heard that a certain mighty man has come and has abode in thy house : bring him unto me." And Tobias came unto Thaddaeus and said to him, " Abgar the Toparch called for me and bade me bring thee to him, in order that thou mightest heal his sickness." And Thaddaeus said, I go up, since I have been sent unto him with might." Tobias therefore, having risen early on the morrow, and taking Thaddaeus with him, came to Abgar. And when he came, suddenly upon his entrance—the king's nobles also being present and standing there—a great sight was manifested to Abgar in the countenance of the apostle Thaddaeus. And when Abgar saw this he worshipped Thaddaeus. Astonishment also fell upon all those that stood by. For they did not see the sight, which appeared to Abgar only. And he asked Thaddaeus, " Art thou in truth a disciple of Jesus the Son of God, who said unto me, 'I shall send to thee a certain one of My disciples, who shall heal thee and give thee life ' ? " And Thaddaeus said, " Since thou hast firmly believed in Him who sent me, therefore was I sent unto thee. And again, if thou believest in Him, according as thou believest the desires of thine heart shall be granted thee." And Abgar said unto him, " I believed in Him so much that I desired to take a force and destroy the Jews who crucified Him, only that I was hindered from doing so by the empire of the Romans." And Thaddaeus said, " Our Lord Jesus hath fulfilled the will of His Father, and having fulfilled it He was received up unto His Father." Abgar saith to him, " I also have believed in Him and in His Father." And Thaddaeus saith, " I therefore lay my hand upon thee in His name." And when he had done this, he was immediately healed of the sickness and the disease which he had. And Abgar marvelled that, according as he had heard concerning Jesus, so had he received in reality from His disciple Thaddaeus, who had healed him without drugs and medicines. And not only so, but Abdus also the son of Abdus, who had the gout.

For the latter also, coming forward, fell at his feet ; and Thaddaeus, having prayed, took him by the hand and healed him. Many others also of their fellow-citizens did the same Thaddaeus heal, doing wondrous and great things, and preaching the Word of God. But after these things Abgar said, " Thou, O Thaddaeus, by the power of God doest these things, and we ourselves marvel at thee. But besides these things I entreat of thee to narrate to me concerning the. advent of Jesus, how it took place, and concerning His power, and by what power He used to do these things of which we have heard." And Thaddaeus said, " I shall be silent for the present, since I was sent to preach the Word. But on the morrow assemble unto me all thy citizens, and unto them I shall preach the Word of God, and I shall sow in them the Word of Life, and shall tell them about the advent of Jesus, how it took place, and about His mission, and why He was sent forth by the Father, and concerning the might of His works, and the mysteries which He proclaimed in the world, and by what power He did these things, and concerning His new proclamation, and concerning His lowliness and humiliation, and how He humbled Himself and died, and how He lessened His divine nature, and was crucified, and descended into Hades, and rent in twain the middle wall of partition which had not been rent from eternity, and raised the dead. For having descended alone, He raised up many with Him unto His Father, and then in this way He ascended." Abgar accordingly gave orders that early on the morrow all his citizens should come together and should hear the preaching of Thaddaeus ; and after these things he commanded to give him gold and treasure. But Thaddaeus would not accept it, saying, " If we have left our own, how shall we accept the things of others ? These things were done in the three hundred and fortieth year' [of the Seleucian Era].

Eusebius adds that the result of Thaddaeus' work at Edessa was the conversion of those that were healed and their admission into the number of Christ's disciples, and states that, in consequence of this, the whole of the people of Edessa had remained Christians even up to his own time *(Eccl. Hist.* ii. 1). This, however, is incorrect : though many were Christians in Eusebius' days.

Armenian writers inform us that Thaddaeus, having thus converted Abgar and his people, baptized them, and then proceeded to erect a large church in the city of Edessa. He also consecrated as bishop of the city a pious convert named Addê, a silkmaker, who had previously been employed to make a royal tiara for Abgar. After his conversion, Abgar, filled with zeal for the Gospel, wrote letters to the Emperor Tiberius and to the Kings of Syria, and to Arṭashês, King of Persia, inviting them to receive the Gospel and accept Christ as their Lord and Saviour. Three years after his conversion Abgar died, and was buried in Edessa (a. d. 35). His widow, Helenê, was also an earnest Christian . When some years later banished from Edessa by Sanatṛouk, she went to her native city, Haran, and there ruled for a time. She is also said to have been Queen of Adiabênê. Somewhat later she went to Jerusalem, and Josephus tells us that, during the great famine in Claudius' time (Acts xi. 28), she bought a great quantity of corn in Egypt and, at enormous expense, had it conveyed to Jerusalem and distributed it to the poor. When she died, a noble tomb was erected to her memory in the suburbs of the Holy City, in memorial of her beneficence.

After founding the Christian Church in Edessa, Thaddaeus went to Armenia proper, to the district of Aṛtaz or Shavaṛshan, which was at that time ruled over by Sanatṛouk, Abgar's sister's son. The latter received him kindly, and gave him every opportunity of preaching the Gospel to the people. As a result of this it is said that Sanatṛouk and his daughter Sandou*kh*t, together with not a few nobles and very many of the common people, were converted and received baptism. Thaddaeus consecrated one of his converts named Zacharias bishop, and it is said that the latter afterwards carried the Gospel to the Alvanians, a tribe living on the shores of the Caspian Sea at the foot of the Caucasus Mountains.

Meanwhile strange things were happening in Edessa itself. The Christians of that city are said to have carried the Gospel into Persia, and the friendship and alliance which existed between Aṛtashês, King of Persia, and Abgar renders this very probable. But on Abgar's death, his son, who is called by different writers Ananias, Ananê, Ananoun and Anan, ascended the throne of Osroênê, and at once apostatized and restored the worship of the heathen gods, especially that of Baal, the great tutelary deity of the city. The temples, which had been closed by Abgar, were reopened, and a certain amount of persecution was begun against the Christians. One instance of this in particular is related. Ananias ordered Bishop Addê, who had made a tiara for Abgar before Thaddaeus' arrival in Edessa, to return to his old trade and make one for him also. Addê refused, saying, 'My hands shall make a tiara for no head which does not bow down to the dust in honour of Christ.' Enraged at this message, Ananias sent the executioner to cut off both the bishop's feet. This was done as he was seated at worship in the church, and resulted in his speedy death.

Meanwhile Sanatṛouk was extending his power in Armenia, and was plotting to make himself master of the throne of Osroênê. Great confusion and disorder followed, but was ended by Ananias' death (a. d. 38) after a reign of only four years. It is said that his death occurred in the following manner. Ananias was having the royal palace in Edessa rebuilt with great magnificence. One day, while standing on the pavement below, surveying the work, a huge marble column fell from the upper story upon the king, striking him to the earth and crushing his legs so severely that he died of the shock. His Christian subjects saw in this event a just judgement upon him for the murder of their good Bishop Addê, and remarked upon the noteworthy circumstance that the king had been smitten upon precisely the same part of the body where Addê had by his orders been struck by the executioner's sword.

Immediately on the news reaching him that Ananias was dead, Sanatṛouk marched to take possession of Edessa. He seems to have already apostatized from the Christian faith, and consequently the Christians of that city at first opposed his entrance. But Sanatṛouk reassured them by binding himself with an oath to permit them the free exercise of their religion. On taking possession of Edessa, Sanatṛouk slew all Abgar's remaining sons, and banished his daughter and his widow, Helenê, to the latters native city, Haran, though he left her the title of Queen of Mesopotamia. We have already learnt the rest of the history of this lady. Having thus removed all rivals from his path, Sanatṛouk felt free to govern according to his own pleasure. He rebuilt in the most splendid manner the city of Nisibis, which had been destroyed by an earthquake, and set up in the public square there a statue of himself with a single drachma in his outstretched hand, implying that he had expended all the rest of his treasures in the work of rebuilding the city.

But Sanatṛouk is famous, or rather infamous, for deeds of a different kind also. In direct contradiction to his oath, he began a most cruel persecution of the Christians, in which he spared neither sex nor age throughout his dominions. Among others that fell victims to the tyrant's fury was Thaddaeus himself. This apostolic man, hearing of Sanatṛouk's apostasy, returned from Cappadocia, whither he had gone to preach the Gospel. On his way to Mesopotamia, it is said, he met five ambassadors sent from Rome to Sanatṛouk's court. One of these was a noble and well-born man named Chrysos. Hearing the Gospel message from Thaddaeus, they accepted it and were baptized. Chrysos himself was ordained presbyter. These men, in the ardour of their new-found faith, sold all that they had and gave to the poor, and then devoted themselves to preaching Christ crucified to the people of Armenia. They seemed to have formed a body of itinerant preachers from among their converts, who lived among the mountains, and who, from the Armenian translation of their original leader's name, were called *Voskeankh,* the ' Golden Ones.' These men for some years continued their work in Armenia, and we shall meet with them again.

Hearing of their conversion, Sanatṛouk summoned Thaddaeus to his presence in Shavaṛshan, where he then happened to be. On the arrival of the apostle, he was martyred with many other devoted Christians, including Sanatṛouk's own daughter, Sandoukht, the first of a noble band of Armenian women who have not feared to lay down their lives for their faith (a. d. 48). Tradition relates that miracles of healing were wrought at Sandoukht's tomb, and that this led to the conversion of many others, not a few of whom wore the martyr's crown. So in all ages and in all lands has the blood of martyrs been the seed of the Church of God.

Later legends add that Bartholomew also came to Armenia in a.d. 50, bringing with him a picture of the Virgin Mary. He is said to have preached in Lower Armenia and to have made many converts, including Sanatṛouk's sister Thakouḥi ('Queen ') and the generalissimo of his army. Sanatṛouk's fury was not appeased by these fresh proofs of the power of the Gospel, which he hated with a renegade's hatred. He put his sister to death, scourged Bartholomew, and then crucified him in the city of Aṛevbanus, where his tomb was long after an object of veneration. Armenian superstition or patriotism claims that the apostle Jude also laboured in that country, and died and was buried at

Urmia. The bones of St. Thomas, the apostle of Parthia and India, were brought from the latter country (where he had been martyred) and interred in Armenia. St. Eustathius, one of our Lord's seventy disciples, was martyred in the province of Siunikh, and buried at a place still called Stathev or Sathev. Elisha, one of Thaddaeus' disciples, accompanied by a little band of three devoted followers, preached, we are told, in Upper Armenia, and then passed on to labour among the Alvanians. He was instrumental in bringing a very large number of these people to a knowledge of the truth, and finally died in the plain of Arghoun. Sanaṭrouk the persecutor reigned for thirty-four years, and having seen the failure of his attempt to crush the infant Christian Church in his dominions, was at last accidentally killed by an arrow while hunting (a.d. 65).

How much or how little of this account of the first preaching of the Gospel in Armenia is true must perhaps forever remain unknown. What we have narrated above is the story as told by Armenian writers for the most part, and believed by them to be correct. A casual glance at such a narrative enables us to see that the historical in it is largely mixed with the legendary. This much, however, is clear, that Christianity was in very early times preached in Armenia, and that many martyrs were produced by the infant Church—names written in the Lamb's Book of Life, though in most instances forgotten among men. In the next chapter we shall clean such other indications of the existence of a living Church in that country before the time of Gregory the Illuminator as the materials at our disposal enable us to adduce.

CHAPTER V

THE INTERVAL BETWEEN THE FIRST AND SECOND PREACHING OF THE GOSPEL

'Fecisti nos ad Te ; et inquietum est cor nostrum, donec requiescat in Te.'—Aug. *Conff.* i. i.

The contest between heathenism and Christianity in Armenia was destined to continue for a few centuries longer. Persecutions recurred at irregular intervals. The disciples of Christ had there, as in other lands, the whole power of the court, the ancient priesthood, and the natural corruption of the human heart to contend with. Ages rolled by before another Christian king sat on the throne and strove, as Abgar had done, to lead his people to Christ. Yet the Gospel leaven continued to spread in men's hearts, and, amid persecutions, trials and afflictions, the work went steadily if quietly forward. Some of the kings, like Eṛvand II, were especially zealous for the heathen gods ; others, like his successor Aṛtashês II (a.d. 85), were brought more or less under Christian influence, and were even thought to incline towards Christianity. Eṛvand II (a.d. 65-85) at one time made the old sacred city of Aṛmavir his capital, and appointed his own son Eṛvand chief of the idol-priests, in order to keep them on his side in political matters. After building the beautiful new city of Eṛvandashat in a commanding position on the west bank of the river Araxes, and making it the capital instead of Aṛmavir, he also built another city, Bagaṛan, forty miles to the north of it on the river Akhouṛean, and erected there the images of the heathen gods from which the new sanctuary derived its name (Bagaṛan = ' Place of the gods ').

When the usurper Eṛvand II was defeated and slain in his own palace by Aṛtashês II, the only surviving son of Sanaṭrouk (a. d. 85), better times at first seemed to have dawned on the Church. Aṛtashês rebuilt Aṛtashat (Artaxata) and made it his capital. Soon after his accession the country was invaded by the Alans and other Caucasian tribes. Aṛtashês defeated them and took their king's son captive. Another more formidable incursion was soon after made by the Alans, in alliance with the Georgians and other neighbouring tribes. The armies met on the banks of the river Kouṛ, the invaders having taken up a position on the left bank and the Armenian forces on the right. A romantic incident then took place, which has been celebrated by Armenian poets and historians. The Alans had demanded the restoration to liberty of their king's son, but this had been refused. Nothing seemed to remain but to appeal to the ordeal of battle, when the captive prince's sister, Sathinik, advanced to the further bank of the river and asked permission to converse with Aṛtashês through an interpreter. Her pleadings for her brother's life and liberty prevailed. Aṛtashês set the prince free, concluded a peace with the invaders, and made their fair princess his queen.

About two years after Aṛtashês' marriage, the Voskean ascetics, who dwelt at Mount Dsaghkê, thought that a favourable opportunity had now come for them to make an attempt to preach the Gospel at court. More than forty years had now elapsed since Thaddaeus' martyrdom, but their leader Chrysos still lived, and himself ventured into the king's presence with the message of salvation. King Aṛtashês seems, according to Thomas Aṛdsṛounî, to have listened with respect to the pious old man, and to have been much inclined to accept Christianity , but his queen was too much devoted to the worship of the goddess Astghik to give ear to the Gospel. Chrysos and his companions, however, were privileged to see their efforts blessed with fruit even at court ; for, though the king ultimately decided to remain a heathen, and had appointed Mazhan, one of his sons, chief of the idol-priests, yet some of Queen Sathinik's kinsmen, who had accompanied her to court, believed in Christ and became candidates for baptism.

After a time the Voskeans returned to their ascetic retreat on Mount Dsaghkê, where they were afterwards joined by these converted Alans, seventeen in number. The new converts were baptized in the waters of the Euphrates, and the chief of them, a nobleman named Baḥadṛas, took in baptism the name of Soukias. The legend says that our Lord appeared to them on the banks of the river, to encourage them to be faithful unto death to the true light which now shone in their hearts. On the spot where the heavenly vision manifested itself to their eyes they erected a cross, which they named the ' Cross of Good News.'

Some fifteen years after this, Aṛtavazd, son of Aṛtashês and Sathinik, accompanied by his brothers, came to the mountain retreat of the Voskeans and endeavoured to prevail upon the Alan converts, his relatives, to return to court and accept once more the religion of the country. When he found that they stood firm, he ordered the Voskeans themselves to persuade them to obey him. The brave and aged Christian ascetics resolutely refused to do as he required, urging that they could not possibly desire any one to deny Christ and return to the worship of idols. This reply aroused the prince's anger against the Voskeans. He commanded his body-guard to put them to death, which was accordingly done.

The Alan converts, who from the name of their leader were called Soukiasians, reverently buried the bodies of their martyred instructors, and then removed to the Jṛaba*kh*t Mountains, better known by the name of the Soukav or Soukavêt Mountains, in the canton "of Bagṛevan. There they dwelt peacefully for some years, living a most ascetic life, and subsisting entirely upon pulse. At last one of the Kings of the Alans, whose name is differently given as Datian or Dikian, commanded one of his nobles to send to them to inquire what deity they worshipped, and to order them to present themselves before him. The noble-man thereupon dispatched an officer and a number of soldiers with instructions to seek out the Soukiasians and compel them—by torture if need be—to come to the court. When the monks received the king's message and understood that he required them to abandon faith in Christ as well as to return to their native land, they refused to do so. They were then cruelly tortured, burning torches being applied to their flesh to compel them to recant. Amid their agonies they praised God, until their persecutors gagged them. Even then they prayed as best they could, beseeching God to have mercy upon Armenia, and enlighten the hearts of its people with the light of the truth of the Gospel. This continued until, despairing of overcoming their Christian courage and endurance, the Alans put them to death. Their bodies were cast into a cave in the vicinity of the place where they suffered. Legend relates, among other wonders, that their bodies remained undecayed for many years in that spot, and that from the cave in which they lay a stream of water flowed forth, which had the most miraculous effects in the healing of disease. In the time of Constantine the Great accident led to the discovery of the corpses of these martyrs, and it is said that the emperor came in person to be present when they were at last interred in a suitable manner. Gregory the Illuminator is related to have been present on this occasion, and to have built a church and established some clergy there, to keep alive the memory of his noble predecessors, the last desire of whose hearts and the prayer uttered with their latest breath he himself had been divinely called to fulfill.

Such martyrdoms as those of the Voskeans and the Soukiasians, far from disheartening the scattered Christians of Armenia, served only to increase their zeal and courage. From that time their numbers continued to grow steadily. The light had begun to dawn, and no power on earth or in hell could extinguish the ray which was destined to grow and flood the whole land. Tertullian informs us that, early in the second century, very many believers in Christ were to be found in Armenia ; and we are told that, in the part of the country which was formed into a Roman province by Trajan (a.d. 9(8-117), many persons suffered martyrdom during his reign.

In Edessa too Christianity continued to make progress. Between A.d. 160 and 170 we learn that the prince who reigned there, Abgar Bar Manu, was a Christian. The famous Syrian Christian writer, Bardesanês, is said to have enjoyed this prince's favour and to have exercised much influence over him ; and we are informed that Abgar forbade under severe penalties the self-mutilation which used to be practised there in honour of the goddess Cybele, and cut off the hands of those found guilty of it. On the coins of Abgar the sign of the cross takes the place of the symbol of Baal which had hitherto appeared there. A Christian church at Edessa, built somewhat after the pattern of the Temple at Jerusalem, is mentioned as in existence as early as A.D. 202.

Among the other few and scattered notices of the existence and spread of Christianity in Armenia before the time of Gregory the Illuminator may be mentioned what Eusebius tells us casually in speaking of Dionysius, Bishop of Alexandria between A.D. 248 and 265. Dionysius was a convert and pupil of Origen, and wrote many letters of advice and instruction to various local Churches in different parts of the world. Eusebius informs us that at that time the Church in Armenia, as in other parts of the world in that age, was governed by bishops, and that Dionysius wrote to the Armenian Church, through its bishop, Merouzanês (in Armenian Meṛou*zh*an), a letter or tractate on the subject of Repentance. Firmilianus also is quoted as stating that, in the time of *Khosṛov* I, who reigned from A.D. 214 to 261, the Christians in Armenia were already so numerous, and were increasing so fast, that the king thought it his duty to persecute them in order to preserve heathenism from utter extinction. Many were massacred, but the persecution was so far from accomplishing its object that his son and successor, Tiridatês III, after in vain publishing most cruel edicts against the Christians, himself yielded to the true faith, and was baptized by St. Gregory the Illuminator (a. D. 302), as we shall see in a subsequent chapter.

In order to understand the state of the country and the political circumstances under which the Christian faith was during all this time carrying on its struggle for existence and ultimate supremacy in Armenia, we must study more in detail the history of the nation and its rulers during the interval that elapsed between Aṛtashês II and the advent of Gregory.

Aṛtashês II, on his death in A.D. 129, was succeeded by his son Aṛtavazd II, whose character afforded a strange contrast to that of his warlike, able and energetic father. Aṛtavazd led a frivolous and luxurious life, the only merit of which consisted in its brevity. He had no children, and therefore selected as his successor his younger brother Tiṛan. driving away from court all the other members of the royal family. His reign lasted only about two years, but his death is involved in some obscurity. According to some authorities he was accidentally killed in hunting by falling into a pit. Other accounts inform us that he suddenly became deranged one day when riding across the bridge over the river Medsamôṛ, a branch of the Araxes, near the city of Aṛtashat, and with his horse leaped into a deep chasm in the ground, and vanished forever from human sight.

His brother Tiṛan I, who succeeded him, lived in the same worthless manner, but his reign lasted from a.d. 131 (probably) until a.d. 151. On the accession of Antoninus Pius to the imperial throne, it is said that Tiṛan sent an ambassador to court to offer his congratulations and pay tribute, besides doing homage in his master's name. Antoninus gave the messenger a very favourable reception, and sent Tiṛan a crown and a *pallium*. We are also told that the emperor caused a medal to be struck, on which he himself was represented with a hand placed upon Tiṛan's shoulder, as if in the act of investing him with the purple, and the inscription ' Rex Armeniis datus V After reigning for about twenty years, Tiṛan confided the government of the country to a satrap named Eṛakhnavi, who had married the widow of King Aṛtavazd, and retired to the district of Ekeghikh, where he spent his time in pleasure. His death was caused by an avalanche, which fell on him when he was out walking (a.d. 151).

Tiṛan also left no children, and was succeeded by his younger brother Tigranês III, who made an effort to shake off the Roman yoke. In alliance with Fìrûz, King of Parthia, Tigranês defeated a Roman army under Severianus, prefect of the province of Cappadocia, and slew their leader. Encouraged by this success, Tigranês marched his army into Asia Minor. There he was by treachery captured and imprisoned by a Greek lady. Meanwhile the Emperor Aurelius had deputed Lucius Verus, his coadjutor in the empire, to put down the rebellion in Armenia. Verus defeated the Armenian forces and subdued the country. On Tigranês' submission, he was then freed from his ignominious captivity and restored to the throne. He is said to have contracted a marriage with a lady named Rophi, one of Verus' relatives, but she did not become his queen, and was ultimately divorced. Her sons were formed into a noble family, who bore the name of Rophseans, but were not reckoned among the Arsacides.

Tigranês died in a.d. 193, and was succeeded by his son Vagharsh, who removed the capital to a city originally called Vaṛtgês, but which, when rebuilt and fortified by this king, was in his honour named Vagharshapat. Among other steps which this monarch took in order to maintain the old and now fast decaying heathenism of Armenia is mentioned the institution of a national religious festival, which was held on the first day of the old Armenian month Navasaṛd (August), which began the ancient Armenian year. Vagharsh's brother Ma*zh*an was high priest of the old religion, and on his death his father, Tigranês, had erected a tomb in his memory, in which was a shrine which served as a place of refuge where fugitives from justice might claim the right of 'sanctuary,' and where they and all comers were fed with the flesh of animals offered in sacrifice. In Vagharsh's time the Sarmatians invaded Armenia, but were met near Darband by the king at the head of his troops, and defeated after a fierce struggle. But Vagharsh himself was wounded by an arrow in the battle, and died of his wound after a reign of twenty years (a.d. 213).

His son, *Khosṛov* I, who succeeded him, is one of the chief figures in Armenian history. Immediately on his accession, *Khosṛov* marched against the turbulent northern tribes for the purpose of avenging his father's death. He crossed the Caucasus, assailed the enemy in their own land, completely defeated them, and erected a statue of himself with an inscription in Greek letters in honour of his victory. He returned to Armenia in triumph, carrying with him as hostages a large number of Sarmatians (a.d. 214). Henceforth *Khosṛov* reigned in peace, until the great revolution in Persia, which overthrew the dynasty of the Arsacides in that country, forced him into a war with Ardashîr, the founder of the Sâsânide dynasty.

The people of Persia proper had long groaned under the tyranny of their Parthian conquerors. The latter, despising the people of the country, endeavoured by oppression to keep them in permanent subjection. But as the original courage and strength of the Parthians gradually yielded to luxury and effeminacy, their common misery bound the Persians together, inured them to hardships, and instilled into their hearts a bitter hatred of their oppressors, which awaited only a favourable opportunity to manifest itself in action. The opportunity at last came, and with it the man needed to make use of it. Artabanus, the last of the Arsacide Kings of Parthia, had by his ingratitude alienated from himself a Persian general named Ardashîr, who claimed descent from one of the ancient Kings of Persia, who had reigned at Istakhr, his birthplace. Ardashîr had gained great repute by his valour in battle, and Artabanus owed to him more than one victory. When banished from court, Ardashîr retired to Persia proper, where he found his fellow-countrymen fully able to sympathize with his wrongs, and wanting only a leader to encourage them to revolt. Placing himself at their head, Ardashîr defeated Artabanus in three great battles, in the last of which —the battle of Hormazd—the Parthian monarch was slain (a.d. 226). Ardashîr was crowned king of the Persian empire at a great national gathering held at Balkh in *Kh*urâsân, and quickly extended his sway over the whole country, until his dominion was bounded by the Euphrates, the Tigris, the Araxes, the Caspian Sea, the Oxus, the Indus and the Persian

Gulf. Being placed on the throne by a Persian revolt, Ardashîr (and in fact the whole Sâsânian dynasty after him) was most zealous for the Magian religion. A great revival of this faith in its later and corrupted form then took place, and lasted until the Muḥammadan conquest of Persia. Every other faith was prohibited throughout the Persian empire, and the Christian Church in Persia during the time of the Sâsânides was called upon to undergo frequent and cruel persecutions, in which thousands of martyrs laid down their lives for their faith.

When *Khosṛov*, King of Armenia, heard of the death of his relative Artabanus IV and the success of Ardashîr's arms, he felt called upon to declare war against the usurper, urged to do so partly by the desire to avenge Artabanus, and partly by that of increasing his own power and asserting his claim to the throne of Persia and the title of ' King of Kings.' Ardashîr's proud defiance hurled in the teeth of the Byzantine empire by his demand that all Roman troops should be instantly recalled from Asia, and that the eastern provinces of the empire should be surrendered to him (a somewhat early foreshadowing of an Oriental 'Monroe Doctrine '), enabled *Khosṛov* to count confidently on the aid of the Romans in his war with Ardashîr. The Romans had during the last half-century extended and consolidated their dominion in Asia. Ctesiphon, founded by the Parthians on the eastern bank of the Tigris, had for some time been considered the capital of that portion of their territory ; but in a.d. 165 this city and Seleucia both fell into the hands of the Romans, by whom they were razed to the ground. In a.d. 198 the Emperor Severus again besieged Ctesiphon, and finally took it by storm. The Romans did not endeavour to retain that part of Mesopotamia, but when they reduced the kingdom of Osroênê to the position of a province, they erected forts in different parts of that territory, and placed a strong garrison in Nisibis. An attempt to shake off the Roman yoke resulted in a speedy conquest of the country, and the last King of Edessa, another Abgar, was carried prisoner to Rome (a.d. 216). Edessa was then made a Roman colony. The strong position which had thus been obtained by the Romans beyond the Euphrates, only ten years before his usurpation of the crown of Persia, probably seemed to Ardashîr to render it imperatively necessary for him to try conclusions with them as soon as he had firmly seated himself upon the throne. He claimed all the conquests of his predecessor Cyrus the Great, and tried to enforce his claim in a war which began in A.D. 233 and lasted, with varying result, not only until the end of his reign, but during those of his son Sapor and more than one of his successors.

Khosṛov, King of Armenia, however, had already declared war against Ardashîr in A.D. 231, or even earlier. All the armies of the Persian empire were unable to accomplish *Khosṛov's* overthrow. His courage and skill, and the devotion and patriotism of his men, aided by fugitives from Persia as well as by the Roman armies, enabled him to maintain for thirty years a fierce struggle with Ardashîr. Finally *Khosṛov* gained more than one victory over the Emperor of Persia, whom (if we may credit Armenian historians) he even compelled to flee for a time to India. However this may be, Ardashîr at last, finding it impossible to overcome *Khosṛov* in the field, determined to accomplish his purpose by treachery. He privately promised an immense reward to anyone who would undertake to murder the Armenian monarch. The King of Armenia, whenever, amid the frequent vicissitudes of its fate, that country was subject to the Persian yoke, enjoyed a rank second only to that of the Persian or Parthian monarch himself. Ardashîr promised to bestow this rank, together with many other honours and rewards, upon any one, gentle or simple, high or low, who would undertake to and succeed in executing vengeance upon *Khosṛov* for the defeats and calamities he had brought upon Persia. This was said solemnly and deliberately at a great meeting of all the ' kings and governors and satraps and captains and chiefs and rulers ' of Ardashîr's realms, held in order to deliberate upon the steps to be taken to overcome *Khosṛov*. ' Perhaps someone may be found who may be able to execute vengeance,' said Ardashîr. ' If so, only in the throne shall I be greater than he.'

There happened to be present at this council a Parthian prince of high rank, a member of the Arsacide family, who bore the name of Anak. On hearing the king's appeal, Anak rose from his seat, and, standing in the midst of the assembly, vowed that he would execute vengeance upon the King of Armenia, even although the latter belonged to the same noble stock as himself. On hearing this, Ardashîr praised the zeal and devotion of Anak, and promised him a crown of gold, lands, wealth and honours more than heart could wish, if he succeeded in carrying his plan into effect.

Anak's treacherous plan was only too successfully executed. On the pretext of fleeing from the tyranny of the usurper Ardashîr, Anak, with his brother, his wife and children, his serfs and all his portable pro-perty, left Persia and made his way into Armenia to the place where the King of Armenia was then lying in winter quarters, at the city of Khaghkhagh in the canton of Outi. *Khosṛov* had been much grieved and disappointed that hitherto so few princes of the Parthian branch of the Arsacide family had joined him, in spite of his appeals to them to assist him in exacting vengeance for the murder of Artabanus. On the contrary, most of them had submitted to Ardashîr, apparently with perfect contentment. Learning therefore of Anak's arrival, *Khosṛov* was prepared to welcome him to his camp ; and this welcome was the more hearty because Anak assured him that he had come to join him in his attempt to punish Ardashîr for the wrongs he had inflicted on the house of Arsacês. To lend more colour to this treacherous plea, Ardashîr had sent a detachment of his army to pursue Anak, and they had kept up the pursuit as far as the frontiers of the province of Atropatenê (Âzarbâijân). *Khosṛov* and the two Parthian princes spent the winter very happily where they were ; and when the spring came, they marched to the city of Vagharṣhapat in the canton of Aiṛaṛat. There *Khosṛov,* in conjunction with these two traitors, planned another of his yearly incursions into the Persian empire. At this distance of time we cannot explain all the facts of the case, nor can we tell why the two conspirators, if they had really, as Agathangelos assures us, come to *Khosṛov* court with the intention of murdering him, took no proper precautions to ensure their own escape and that of their families from the vengeance of the Armenians. Sufficient to say that, one day during the chase, the two brothers, taking the king aside, apparently to converse about some plan for amusement or matter of business, plunged their swords in his breast and laid him lifeless at their feet (a.d. 261). Before the king's officers and courtiers could realize the crime which had been committed, Anak and his brother mounted their horses and fled.

The Armenian generals acted with great promptness in this emergency. Knowing that the river Araxes was then flooded, owing to the melting of the snows in the upper part of its course, they decided that the only chance of escape which the murderers had was to make for the bridge at the city of Aṛtashat (Artaxata), not many miles away. To prevent this they sent a detachment of cavalry to hold the far end of that bridge, and pursued the fugitives until, on the bridge itself, hemmed in on both sides, the latter halted and fought for their lives. The struggle was soon over, and in a few moments the corpses of the traitors were being swept along by the turbulent current of the swollen Araxes. *Khosṛov,* after receiving his death-stroke, had rallied for an instant, long enough to enjoin upon his officers with his latest breath the duty of annihilating the whole family of his murderers. This command they vowed to obey.

Then began a slaughter great and cruel. Anak's wife, children and relatives were massacred without mercy and without distinction of sex or age. Only two of the whole body escaped—a little boy who was about three years of age at the time, and his brother, a few years older. The elder child was named Souṛên : he was carried off by his rescuers to the Persian court, where he was brought up to the profession of arms under the care of his paternal aunt, and ultimately became a distinguished warrior. The younger child had been born to Anak during his residence in Vagharshapat, according to one account, or, as others say, on his journey from Persia, in the year 257. He owed his escape from the massacre to the fidelity of his nurse Sophia and her brother Euthalius, both Christians of Greek descent. Though the child's mother, Ogohi, perished in the massacre, his nurse succeeded in escaping with her little charge to Caesarea in Cappadocia. The child thus wonderfully preserved is the greatest figure in the whole history of Armenia, for hc ultimately grew up to be the brave, patient, devoted ' Apostle of Armenia,' St. Gregory the Illuminator.

When the Persian monarch heard of the success of his nefarious plot and the death of *Khosṛov,* he at once marched an army into Armenia. The Armenian nobles bravely resisted his advance, and were supported by the Roman forces, which marched from Phrygia to their aid. After a fierce struggle, however, Ardashîr routed his opponents with great slaughter. Many of the Armenian nobles fell into his hands, and the rest either shut themselves up in their fortresses or fled to the Roman empire. The family of the ill-fated *Khosṛov* were captured and put to the sword by the conqueror, except two, a youth named Tṛdat (Tiridatês) and his sister *Khosṛovi*dou*kh*t. The latter owed her escape to the loyalty of a nobleman called Ota Amatouni, who carried her off to the impregnable fortress of Ani, where he held out until the restoration of the Armenian monarchy. The young Prince Tiridatês was rescued from Ardashîr's hands by another Armenian noble, Aṛtavazd Mandakouni, who fled with Tiridatês to Rome, where the young prince was brought up and trained in all manly and warlike exercises. But Aṛtavazd's fidelity cost him dear, for the Persian monarch, learning of Tiridatês' escape, massacred the whole of his family and relatives except one of his sisters, whom Tachat, chief of Ashots, helped to make good her escape to Caesarea, where he married her.

The whole of Armenia had now fallen into Ardashîr's hands. The Emperor Valerian and his immediate successors, though anxious to check the advance of the Persians, were prevented from doing so by a Scythian invasion of the empire and by civil disturbances. The Emperor Tacitus did march against the Persians, but suffered a defeat. Probus made peace, recognizing Armenia as a Persian province, which it continued to be until a. d. 287. Ardashîr released the Armenian nobles whom he had taken prisoners, and restored them their lands and privileges on condition of their remaining faithful to himself. He obliterated the inscriptions of Aṛtashês II, and caused his own name to be inscribed in Persian in their stead. He showed his zeal for the Magian religion by breaking many of the idols which the heathen Armenians worshipped, and commanding that the fire sacred to Ôrmazd should be kept constantly burning in the temple at Bagavan. Ardashîr fixed the amount of taxation, and introduced in both Persia and Armenia such admirable laws that, in the former country at least, they commanded the respect of the people until the Arabian conquest. He reigned over both countries till his death, and was succeeded by his son Sapor I, who had previously been associated with his father in the sovereignty of the whole Persian empire.

CHAPTER VI

ARMENIAN MANNERS AND CUSTOMS UNDER THE ARSACIDES

' Sed tu, quamvis caussam tantae dispositionis ignores, tamen, quoniam Bonus mundum Rector temperat, recte fieri cuncta ne dubites.'— Boëthius, *De Cons. Phil.* iv. 5.

In our own day and generation it has come to be understood that the history of a nation does not consist solely in accounts of the wars waged by its kings, in the narrative of their pomp and magnificence, their greatness and their decline, but much more truly concerns itself with the life and habits of the nation over whom they reigned and for whose benefit they held their high estate. In endeavouring to understand, therefore, the circumstances under which Christianity entered and gradually pervaded Armenia, it is not enough to detail the historical facts that we have briefly recounted in previous chapters. We require to learn also all that we can regarding the state of the country in general, the laws and institutions therein established, the condition of society, the degree of civilization attained, and the religious ideas of the people. This last subject we have already considered. We now proceed to learn what is known regarding the condition of Armenia in all secular matters during the rule of the Arsacide dynasty of kings, under whom, after a struggle extending over several centuries, Armenia became a professedly Christian country at an earlier date than any other country in the world.

In Armenia, as in Persia, the constitution of the country under the Arsacides was what may be described as an Aristocratic Monarchy. The kingdom was hereditary. The power of the sovereign was in great measure limited by the nobility. The latter formed an aristocratic caste as ancient as the nation itself. When, however, Vagharṣhak, the founder of the Arsacide dynasty in Armenia, ascended the throne, he re-established the nobility in the privileges which, during the preceding period of anarchy and bloodshed, they had in some measure lost, and increased their power and influence. But at the same time he rendered them dependent on the crown in a manner which no previous period had seen. The former sovereigns of Armenia had constantly found the nobles jealous of their independence, and liable to rebel at any moment against the king. All previous attempts to establish a strong central government had been in vain. But Vagharṣhak determined to render the nobles a support and defence, instead of remaining a source of weakness and danger to the crown. It is to his success in this attempt that Armenia owed her time of greatest prosperity, and was enabled to preserve any measure of autonomy amid the constant wars that raged between the more powerful nations which surrounded her, and which often desired to make Armenia their battle-field.

The system established by Vagharṣhak was by no means unlike the feudal system in Europe. The king became the fountain of honour, and all estates were held on titles given by him. He secured to the nobility all the rights and privileges they had formerly enjoyed, but in return imposed certain obligations upon them, so as to bind them to the court. The whole body of the nation were divided into two great classes called respectively the 'free ' or noble and the ' unfree ' or common people. The nobles themselves were again divided into two orders, the 'greater' and the ' lesser ' barons. To the former the sovereign granted the ' honour and dignity of greatness,' i.e. the privilege of sitting on a cushion in the king's presence, which no others enjoyed. But there were also grades of rank among the greater barons, distinguished by the titles 'first throne,' 'second throne,' &c. In former times all the nobles were territorial lords, but Vagharṣhak introduced the practice of raising men to the rank of noble in virtue of their position at court, without in every case assigning to them landed estates. The landed nobility, however, had certain special privileges, of which the principal were the following:—(1) They ruled their ancestral demesnes in a measure independently of the king; (2) They judged their tenants with the power of life and death ; (3) They levied taxes on them at their own will ; (4) They might maintain bodies of troops levied from among their own retainers or serfs. But in return for these rights and privileges the nobles owed allegiance to the king, and were bound (1) to aid the king with their forces in case of war, and (2) to pay him taxes or tribute. When these duties were not performed, trouble naturally arose ; but as a general rule they were discharged faithfully enough when the sovereign had power to enforce them. The landed nobility were called 'lords,' ' houselords,' or even ' patriarchs' ; both the latter titles showing how ancient the order was, and what was its origin.

Vagharṣhak's code divided the commonalty also into two orders, called respectively ' citizens ' and 'villagers' or *town* and *country* people. The latter were commanded to honour the ' citizen ' class as their chiefs or masters. The taxes pressed exclusively upon these unfortunate serfs, who had to supply all that was needed for the maintenance of two separate courts, those of the king and of their immediate feudal lord. It is not surprising, therefore, to learn that the ' villagers ' were gradually deprived of land, while most of the wealth of the country had a tendency to accumulate in the hands of a small body of individuals.

Vagharṣhak's successors increased the number of noble houses, principally for the purpose of rewarding valour in battle. In such cases they often assigned estates also to their favourites. Only after the introduction of Christianity, however, do we find the king punishing rebellious nobles by confiscating their estates in favour of those whom he deemed likely to be faithful, and who had deserved well at his hands.

The Arsacide monarchs kept enormous armies in the field, in order to preserve the country from foes external and internal. The forces which Aṛtashês I is said to have maintained were fabulously large. Plutarch estimates the army of Tigranês II at 260,000 men, while others double or treble this estimate. After the accession of Aṛtavazd I, the political unity of the country was for a time broken, and the military power in consequence was much reduced. But Aṛtashês II and *Khosṛov* I must both have maintained large forces. These, however, were not like the standing armies of modern days, for they seem for the most part to have consisted of hastily raised levies from various tribes, not easily brought to obey one leader, almost without discipline, and ill-armed. At the end of a campaign they were for the most part dismissed to their homes, to be called together again only when actually needed. All this prevented the enormous hosts assembled from being effective when matched against a small but well-armed and trained body of Roman troops. Aṛtashês II and Tigranês II gained victories over other Asiatic princes and their armies, but could do little against the legions of Rome. Lucullus had only 20,000 men at the battle of Tigranocerta, yet he completely routed Tigranês' immense host. Aṛtashês II twice repelled the attacks of the Caucasian tribes, but he was soon obliged to submit to Trajan's comparatively small but well-disciplined army. It is curious to notice how history repeats itself. In all times, ancient and modern—as the history of the English empire in India exemplifies—Oriental armies of immense size have, by their very numbers, been rendered helpless and turned into armed mobs in hopeless rout before vastly smaller European *armies,* properly so called. The only really formidable portion of the Armenian army, in the estimation of the Romans, was the light cavalry. These were very similar to those of the Parthians, and fought in the same way, by pretending to flee and discharging a flight of arrows and darts upon their pursuers, and then turning upon them when least expecting a rally. Against the Roman legions in the open field, however, even the Armenian cavalry were powerless. The Armenians had bravery enough, but followed the usual Eastern tactics too blindly to be even able successfully to defend their country against Western invaders, though the natural defences of the land might, with more sensible and reasonable tactics, have rendered Armenia as fatal to an invading host as was Russia to Napoleon's ill-fated army. The chief weapons of the Armenian soldier were the spear, the sword, and above all the bow. The arrow-head was often so constructed as to come off and remain in the wound, and thus prevent extraction.

The ' Border regiments,' maintained for the defence of the marches, are specially worthy of notice, as they approached more nearly to a modern standing army than any other part of the host. They were under specially selected commanders, though the whole army was under the command of a generalissimo or marshal, who bore the title of Spaṛapet or Miakl*khapet.* To Vaghaṛshak is due the institution of the Border regiments. In after times, though their maintenance was occasionally intermitted, it was always found necessary to restore such a force. The various regiments in the army were distinguished by the names of cantons or provinces or offices of dignity, as e.g. the *Aiṛaṛatean* and the *Maṛapetakan* regiments.

The Arsacide monarchs were distinguished for their great love of building cities. Sometimes these were built with a political object, at others merely for the king's pleasure, for a summer or winter residence, as the case might be, or as a royal city, or even for the purpose of perpetuating the sovereign's own name. Hardly a single king of this dynasty can be named who did not indulge in this pastime.

The Arsacides were, as a rule, passionately devoted to hunting, a pastime which they doubtless borrowed from the Parthians, and the latter from the Assyrians. Xenophon tells us that the Persian kings used the chase as an exercise to train their own and their nobles' sons for the battle-field. In order to facilitate hunting, the royal parks and forests were carefully planted, walled round and stocked with game of various kinds.

Besides this absolutely necessary training in manly sports, such of the Arsacide princes as had any natural tendency towards study were given a good education in the language and literature of Greece. It is a well-known fact that most of the sovereigns of this dynasty had a special love for the Greek language, religion, art, customs and civilization. Nor is this remarkable when we consider the immense and widespread influence that, after the conquests of Alexander, the Greek world exercised over the East, from Aethiopia to the Caucasus, and from the Mediterranean to the Indus and the borders of China. For centuries Greek was the *Lingua Franca* of the ancient world, and almost the only language of commerce, diplomacy and learning alike. The Arsacide monarchs were specially proud of the title of *φιλελλήν,* and the inscriptions on their coins are in large measure Greek. Tigranês II's palace was adorned with fine theatres, where Greek tragic dramas were represented by Hellenic actors. Plutarch tells us that great friendship existed between Orodês, King of Parthia, and Aṛtavazd, Tigranês' son. They used to give banquets to one another, at which Greek poems were usually recited, for Orodês was well acquainted with the Greek language and literature, while Aṛtavazd had composed various stories, speeches and tragedies in that tongue. When Crassus' head was brought to Tigranês' palace, Aṛtavazd and Orodês wrote a tragedy on his fate in Greek, and caused it to be acted in their presence. A little later Sapor I, the second monarch of the Sâsânian dynasty in Persia, was celebrated for his knowledge of Greek, and, as Abu'l Fidâ informs us, translated from that language into Persian all the works of the Greek philosophers that he could obtain.

Although so much attached to Hellenism, the Arsacides retained many of their ancestral manners and customs. Among these polygamy must be specially noted. Originally polygamy must have been as completely alien to Armenian ideas and habits as to those of all other Âryan nations of ancient as well as modern times, if we except, perhaps, the Hindus. The Arsacides probably were the first to introduce the practice into Armenia, and they were after a time imitated by some of the nobles, but not by the people in general. The Armenians have always been distinguished for the purity of their family life ; and some of their writers conclude, from the narrative of Semiramis and their ancient hero Aṛa, who refused the guilty queen's amorous overtures, and died in battle against her rather than yield and so disgrace his wife and family, that even among their kings in ancient days any licence of that kind was unknown. But it certainly was permitted under the Arsacides ; and these monarchs were so much in favour of polygamy that they continued to practise it even after the country had accepted Christianity as the national religion. Yet even in heathen times the Arsacide monarch had one wife who held a position far superior to that of the rest. She was called the ' Queen,' or the ' Head of the Wives,' or the ' Lady ' *par excellence,* and stood entirely apart from the rest in dignity. When the king made a lady his ' Queen,' her name was solemnly enrolled in the list of the Arsacide family ; she was robed in the royal purple like the king himself, and a crown was placed on her head. The narrative of the nuptials of King Aṛtashês II and Princess Sathinik, which is perhaps somewhat coloured by poetic fancy, states that, after the marriage ceremony, when the royal pair reached the palace gates, the king scattered gold among the people, while the queen showered down pearls on her attendants as she entered the nuptial chamber.

The funerals of the kings and of the greater nobles were performed with great pomp and magnificence. Aristo of

Pella, who was an eye-witness of the obsequies of Aṛtashês II, is quoted as giving the following description of the ceremony. The coffin, he tells us, was of gold, and the funeral couch of *byssus.* Over the corpse was cast a coverlet interwoven with gold. On the head was a crown. Golden armour was borne in front of the body. Around the bier stood the king's sons and numerous relatives. Behind them attendants in full armour were marshalled, together with satraps of noble family, numerous nobles and officers of the army, all in armour and drawn up in battle array. Trumpets sounded in front of the procession, and behind it followed wailing maidens and mourning women, attired in sorrowful apparel. Last of all there came a crowd of the common people.

The old custom of uttering cries of despair and singing mournful songs at funerals, which was natural enough before the bright light of the Gospel dissipated the gloom which encircled the tomb, still continued in Armenia after the introduction of Chris-tianity, and cannot be said to have entirely died out even now. The sad notes of the *pandura,* and trumpet, and other musical instruments accompanied the lamentations of the professional female mourners, whose tales of the sorrows of the departed moved the tears of those present. The grief of the relatives of the deceased was without limit—at least in its expression. They used to pluck out their hair by the roots, beat their breasts, tear their faces with their nails, and in fact manifest their sorrow by all the other usual unrestrained Oriental methods of lamenting. Men and women, dancing a solemn religious dance, used to circle round the bier clapping their hands, this being another sign of grief.

In speaking of the religion of ancient Armenia we have already remarked that Tigranês II and Aṛtashês I introduced into the country the images of Grecian deities. These, however, being identified with the corresponding local deities, were worshipped in the same manner as had previously been usual in Armenia. The priests formed a separate class of the people, as the office was at first confined to the family of Vaḥagn, who were hence called Vaḥouneans. But Tigranês II deprived them of the priesthood ; and after that persons of other families were appointed to it, among them, as we have seen, being more than one prince of the royal family itself. The priests, like the feudal nobles, were permitted to maintain their own armed retainers, who formed what was known as the ' army of the priests.' They had also lands appropriated to their use and called the ' land of the priests.'

The question as to the existence of an indigenous literature in Armenia before the time of Mesṛop, the inventor of the present Armenian alphabet, is an interesting one, but only a very imperfect answer can be given to it. From the number of cuneiform inscriptions found in various parts of the country, it is evident that in comparatively early times the Armenians were acquainted with this form of writing, originally derived from Babylonia. It may fairly be deduced from the language of Moses of *Khoṛenê* on the subject, that the Zend alphabet[1] was used, at least in the royal archives, and was probably introduced with the rise of the Arsacide monarchy in Armenia. If so, the Zend characters then in use must have been very much of the same kind as those used, e.g., in the inscription on the tomb of Sapor III (a.d. 384-389), and not the much-improved and beautiful alphabet now known as that of the Avesta. The Greek, Latin and Syriac alphabets were also well known in the country ; but none of them was at all well suited to express the sounds of the Armenian tongue. The only libraries mentioned were those stored in the temples and in the kings' palaces. The former con-sisted wholly of religious records kept by the idol-priests, and were called the 'Temple Chronicles' or the ' Temple History.' The most important of these was preserved in the ancient fortress of Ani. Any civil or political events that were mentioned in these priestly records were viewed wholly from their religious aspect ; and the result must have borne a striking likeness to certain ancient Anglo-Saxon chronicles drawn up in the monasteries of England in more recent times. The Arsacide kings had special scribes appointed to compose and preserve in the royal libraries a chronological account of their exploits. These, being contemporary documents, must have been of great value, if they were not indited with the fearful amount of flattery which Oriental monarchs usually expect from their court historians. In Persia also such chronicles were kept, and in both countries they were designated the ' Chronicles of the Kings.' All important documents relating to treaties with foreign states, title-deeds of estates, and royal decrees and laws, were also preserved in the royal libraries. We learn from Moses of Khoṛenê that both the religious and the royal archives existed in his time (his work ends about a.d. 440), and he made extensive use of both. It is clear that the literature of Armenia before the establishment of Christianity in the country was not very extensive, and what there was of it has entirely perished, if we except the information drawn from these chronicles by Moses of Khoṛenê and perhaps a few other writers of early Christian times. There was nothing to give promise of the great abundance of historians, poets, translators and literary men of almost every description that Armenia has produced ever since Christianity gave a new and nobler impulse to the genius and natural ability of the Armenian people.

CHAPTER VII

TIRIDATÊS, GREGORY, AND THE MARTYRDOM OF RHIPSIMÊ

' Mi pghdsestsen zanoun souṛb Kho ḥethanoskh. Dou kaṛogh es phṛkel zis i pghdsouthenês haismanê ; zi vakhchanetsaits sṛboutheamb meranel vasn anouand Kho medsi.'—Rhipsimê's prayer: Agathangelos, *Patm.* kl. 16.

'Let not the heathen defile Thy holy Name. Thou art able to deliver me from this pollution ; so that I may end by dying in holiness for the sake of Thy great Name.'

THE time had now come for the final triumph of Christianity in Armenia. The hour was about to strike, and the man had been born who, in God's good Providence, was destined to complete the work which, ever since our Lord's own time, devoted men and women had been labouring to accomplish in that land, and it often seemed toiling in vain. But the leaven was working steadily, and the Church was about to come forth from prisons and dens and caves of the earth and seat herself upon the throne of the Arsacides.

To human ken things seemed at their worst. The Persian throne was filled by a mighty warrior, Sapor I, who belonged to a dynasty in the highest degree inimical to Christianity, and who strove to quench the flames of Christian faith and zeal throughout all his extensive realms in the blood of the soldiers of the Cross. The ancient Zoroastrianism of Persia, to all appearance for centuries past almost dead, had risen as if from the tomb, and, in the form of Magianism, was boldly and mercilessly asserting its right to rule wherever the Persian monarchs held sway. The persecution of the Christians in Armenia had been recommenced by *Khosṛov*, and his Persian foe Ardashîr had continued the fell undertaking, and confided the prosecution of it to his son. In the Roman empire Diocletian and his coadjutors in the East raged with merciless fury against the Church, and, in all else opposed to the Persians, were in this one point their allies. In neither of the two great empires, which then disputed with one another the sovereignty of the world, could a Christian hope to live a peaceful life or rest at last in a bloodless grave. The heir to the Armenian throne, the youthful Tiridatês (Tṛdat), then serving in the Roman army, had already shown himself to be full of zeal for the gods and of hatred of the Christian name. His strength of body and valour of heart were equalled by his firmness of will ; and the scattered Christians of Armenia, in spite of all their trust in God, may well have trembled at the thought of the fate in store for them and their dear ones when their rightful king should ascend the throne of his fathers. Yet ' the darkest hour is just before the dawn': and the time had nearly come when Armenia should as a nation turn to Christ, and justly claim the honour of being the first of all the nations of the world to accept Christianity as the established religion of the land.

As we have seen in a previous chapter, when *Khosṛov* was murdered, his little son Tiridatês was saved from meeting a like fate at the hands of the Persian invader Ardashîr by the faithfulness of an Armenian noble, Aṛtavazd Mandakouni, who fled with him to Rome. The young prince was there brought up in the family of a certain Count Licianês or Licinius, and early distinguished himself by great feats of strength and by his dauntless courage. We are told that he took part in the Olympic games[1] and won the much coveted wreath of wild olive, the prize of the victor. The fables related about him by Armenian writers are endless. We are told that on one occasion he fought with a wild bull, having no weapon but his enormous strength. Seizing his savage opponent by one horn, he pulled it out, and then slew the animal by twisting its neck. While contending in a race at Rome, he was by an accident thrown out of his chariot. Pursuing the fleeing horses, he stopped them in full career by seizing with his hands the rear part of the chariot. His prowess in war was as remarkable as in the stadium. In a battle with the Goths he saved the life of his patron Licinius. Again, when the Roman legionaries rose in revolt and murdered their ill-fated Emperor Probus, Tiridatês stood at the entrance to Licinius' tent and prevented the mutineers from entering (a.d. 282). In the disastrous struggle between Carus and the Persians in Mesopotamia, when the Romans were defeated and the legions completely routed, Tiridatês, having had his steed killed under him, placed the horse's trappings and his armour on his own back, and in this condition swam across the Euphrates and rejoined the remains of the army on the other side (a. d. 284). During one of Diocletian's battles with the Goths, we are told, the king of the barbarians, a giant of great strength (named, as some writers inform us, Ḥrchhê), came forth between the armies and challenged Diocletian to a single combat, on the issue of which should rest the fate of both nations. By Licinius' advice the emperor gladly availed himself of Tiridatês' offer to accept the challenge in his stead. Disguising himself in the imperial robes, the young Armenian hero met and defeated his gigantic adversary, and brought him captive to the feet of Diocletian. It is said that, when the emperor heard who the brave young warrior was, and learnt that he was the rightful heir to the throne of Armenia, to the suzerainty of which country the Romans, ever since Nero's time, had laid claim, he at once resolved to restore him to his inheritance. Clothing Tiridatês in the royal purple and placing a crown upon his head, he sent him with a Roman army to recover the throne of the Armenian Arsacides.

When, in A. d. 286, Tiridatês reached Caesarea in Cappadocia, he was instantly joined by many of the leading Armenian nobles, who, by the hand of Smbat Bagṛatouni, one of the principal of their number, placed the crown of Armenia on his brow. Advancing into his native land, he was everywhere received with general acclamations of delight. At the ancient fortress of Ani he was joined by his sister *Khosṛovidoukht* and her brave guardian and preserver, Ôta Amatouni, who had held out gallantly in that city against the Persians for twenty-six years. The royal treasures which Ôta had preserved aided Tiridatês very considerably in his war for the recovery of the throne. He conferred on Ôta the rank of Hazaṛapet or Chiliarch, but appointed Aṛtavazd Mandakouni general-in-chief of Armenia. The internal dissensions which then rent the Persian empire, the restorer of which, the great Ardashîr, had recently died, enabled Tiridatês in a comparatively short time to expel the Persians from the whole of Armenia, and even to carry the war into the enemy's country. His exploits at this time caused Tiridatês' fame as a warrior to spread far and near ; and Agathangelos informs us that this gave rise to a proverb, by which any impetuous fiery hero was said to be ' Like the haughty Tiridatês, who with his proud stride overthrew the embankments of rivers, and even

dried up the whirlpools of the seas in his onward march.'
Having succeeded in recovering Armenia from the Persians. Tiridatês, having the desire to ally himself with the chief of the Caucasian nations, who had on previous occasions aided the enemies of the country, sent Smbat Bagṛatouni to demand for him in marriage the hand of Ashkhên, daughter of Ash*kh*aṛad or Ash*kh*adaṛ, King of the Alans. *Ashkhên* accordingly became Queen of Armenia, as her fellow-countrywoman Sathinik had been some generations before.
When Narsês succeeded in making himself master of the whole of Persia in A. D. 294, and in thus putting an end to the long-continued disturbances which had weakened that empire, he renewed the war with Tiridatês. On this occasion the Persians were successful, and Tiridatês was compelled to flee to Constantinople, while Armenia again submitted to the Sâsânian yoke. Diocletian and Galerius warred with the Persians in Mesopotamia in 297, but the Roman army was utterly defeated near the spot memorable for the rout of Crassus in earlier times. In 298 Galerius renewed the struggle, on this occasion choosing Armenia as the battle-field. The Persian army was surprised and cut to pieces. Narsês himself was nearly captured, and had to seek safety in flight. The rout was so complete that Narsês sued for peace, and accepted the terms dictated by the Romans. Tiridatês was restored to his throne, and for many years peace reigned in the country. This gave the requisite opportunity for the preaching of the Gospel and the conversion of Tiridatês and his people to faith in Christ. To understand, however, how this great work was accomplished, we must return to the period immediately succeeding the murder of *Khosṛov*, and trace the history of one of the two surviving sons of Anak, his Parthian friend and murderer.
Gregory was born, as the best accounts relate, in a.d. 257 in the city of Vagharshapat, where his father Anak was then dwelling for a time. He was entrusted to the care of a Christian nurse, Sophia, a Greek of Caesarea, who had married a Persian named Bourdar, and had come with him and her own brother, Euthalius, on a visit to Vagharshapat. When the Armenian nobles, at *Khosṛov's* dying request, ordered all Anak's family to be put to the sword (a.d. 261), Euthalius succeeded in concealing his sister Sophia and her foster-child for a time, and, when the storm had passed, he took them to Caesarea. A fable of later origin assures us that, on the journey, while nurse and child rested under a tree, an angel in the form of a dove alighted on its branches above the child's head, and in a melodious voice addressed him by the name Gregory, which was therefore afterwards given to him in baptism. The boy was brought up in Caesarea as a Christian, and was well instructed in the Scriptures and in the Greek and Syriac languages. When he had grown up, he married a maiden named Mariam, daughter of an Armenian who bore the name of David. Both were Christians, and must naturally have told Gregory something of the deplor-able heathenism of their native land and of the brave martyrs who had already been the first fruits of Armenia to Christ. Of this marriage two sons were born, the elder named Vṛthanês and the younger Aṛistakês. Three years after their marriage, it is said, Gregory and his wife parted by mutual consent. She entered a nunnery at Caesarea, taking her younger son with her. Gregory entrusted to guardians the training and education of the elder, and himself went to Rome to enter the service of the youthful prince Tiridatês (a.d. 280), hoping by faithful and devoted service in some measure to atone to *Khosṛov's* son for the crime which Anak had committed, and of which and his own connexion with the perpetrator Gregory had until very recently been kept in complete ignorance.
His two sons were both spared to grow up to man's estate. Aṛistakês was taught by a hermit, Nicomachus, in the desert, and grew up a recluse. Vṛthanês, on the other hand, remained in the world, married, and had two sons, Gṛegoṛis and Housik. We shall meet with them all at a later period.
Entering Tiridatês' service, Gregory, by his fidelity and loyal obedience, rapidly acquired his master's confidence and esteem. In Tiridatês' eyes he had only one fault, his devotion to the cause of Christ. Tiridatês, even before he returned to Armenia to take possession of the throne of his fathers, made several attempts by promises and threats to induce Gregory to renounce Christianity ; but his non-success in these attempts did not prevent him from permitting his devoted adherent and valued servant to accompany him to Armenia in a.d. 286. Of Gregory's parentage he was in complete ignorance.
During the first year of his reign, when he was in the first flush of victory, Tiridatês resolved to return thanks for his success to the goddess Anahit, who was entitled the great daughter of the god Aṛamazd, and was regarded by the Armenians as the tutelary goddess and the very ' life ' of their native land. He accordingly marched into the canton of Ekeghikh , and reached the village of Eṛiza, where a most renowned temple of the goddess stood, pitching his camp on the banks of the river Gail (Lycus). One day, after a great banquet, in which he had become greatly excited by the wine which he drank, the king commanded Gregory to take the flowers off the royal table and, weaving them into garlands, to present them together with green boughs on the altar of the ' Golden Mother,' as Anahit, among other titles, was called. Gregory respectfully but firmly declined to do so, urging his worship of the only True God as his reason for declining to obey the first order of the king which he had ever been unable to execute. At this the king, urged on by his pride, and probably also by the presence of the heathen priests and the officers of his army, said to him : ' You, a stranger and a man without a country, have come and joined us ; how, then, do you dare to worship a God whom I do not worship ? ' He then ordered Gregory to be imprisoned, and brought before him again the next day. This was done.
Agathangelos, the contemporary historian, who wrote a life of Gregory, gives us a graphic account of the scene which took place when the Christian hero, destined to be the Illuminator of Armenia, on the following day stood before the heathen king as the champion of the Gospel. Alone and unfriended, he felt that he was not alone, because it was given him to realize his Master's presence with him, and to rely upon Him for strength to help in time of need. And He whose strength is made perfect in weakness did not fail His servant in his extreme need.

Tiridatês began by speaking kindly and in terms of regard and affection to Gregory : ' For many years past,' said he, ' I have observed thee, and thou hast with singleness of mind served me with all thine heart. I was pleased with thine endeavours, and had it in mind to prosper thee exceedingly. Why, then, dost thou not perform my desire ? '

Gregory replied, ' It has been commanded by God that servants should be obedient to their masters according to the flesh, as thou dost testify concerning me that I have served thee with all my might. But it is not proper to give to any one the honour and worship due to God, for He alone is the Creator of heaven and earth, and of the angels who laud His majesty, and of men who were created by Him. And it is their duty to worship Him and to do His will, as must all else that is in the sea and on the dry land.'

The king threatened to inflict on him dishonour and disgrace, to cast him into prison, and even to put him to death, if he still persisted in his refusal to worship the gods of the country, especially the ' Great Lady Anahit, the glory and life-giver of my nation, whom all kings honour, and especially the Emperor of Rome : for she is the Mother of all sobriety and virtue, the fortress of the whole human race, and the offspring of the Great and Good Aṛamazd.' But he promised to give him honour, noble rank, wealth, life, if he would yield to his wishes in the matter.

Nothing daunted, Gregory said, ' If thou expel me from this life, thou dost send me to the joy which Christ has prepared for me.' He continued in this tone, with great boldness showing the vanity of idol-worship, and the certainty that those who suffer for

Christ here will after death live again with Him, appealing to the Holy Scriptures and to the fact of Christ's resurrection for the proof that his conviction of this was well founded, and ending with a proclamation of the approaching return of Christ in His glory.

The king asked in contempt, ' Who is this Christ of thine ? Will He loose thy bonds ? ' When after a long argument Gregory showed no signs of submis-sion, the king commanded him to be cruelly tortured until he should give way. Agathangelos gives a most fearful account of the awful sufferings which the soldier of the Cross most bravely endured day after day and week after week. But, though frequently brought into the royal presence and invited to recant, Gregory persisted in his fidelity to Christ. At last, when the king was endeavouring to devise still more exquisite tortures, he was informed by Aṛtavazd Mandakouni, on the authority of Tachat, chief of Ashots, that the latter had just recognized Gregory as the son of Anak the Parthian, who was the murderer of Tiridatês' father *Khosṛov*.

Nothing could exceed the wrath of the king when he heard these words. Gregory's sentence was quickly pronounced. There was in the city of Aṛtashat, in the canton of Aiṛaṛat, a fearful *oubliette* of enormous depth under the castle ; and this was used, according to Agathangelos, as the living tomb of all criminals sentenced to death in the whole country. Such unfortunate wretches were lowered down into this awful dungeon and left there to die of starvation, having as their companions, besides the rotting carcases of those who had previously shared the same fate, the noxious creatures bred amid the inconceivable abominations of their prison. Into this Tiridatês commanded Gregory to be cast. With fetters on hands and feet, and even on his neck, Gregory was forced to march from Eṛiza to Aṛtashat, where he was let down into the dungeon and left to perish there of hunger.

Later writers narrate a story here which, though it may very possibly be fabulous, is not devoid of interest, and shows something of the state of men's minds in Armenia at the time to which it refers. It is said that, when being dragged along to prison and to death, Gregory arrived one day at a village called Souṛên. There he met a company of Christian Armenians, who came and fell at his feet. These were the patients at a hospital which Souṛên, chief of the canton of Salaḥounikh, had built there eight years before for the reception of the sick, among whom his only son Athenagoṛos *was* numbered. Souṛên and his wife Aghvithas, with their son, had taken up their abode there near a fountain called Aṛbenout, where they had built their hospital, and gradually received into it as many as thirty sick folk, among whom there happened to be a Christian presbyter named Dasios. In spite of his weakness and sufferings, Dasios had earnestly and faithfully preached Christ crucified to his companions in misery, and with such success that they all, except Souṛên, Aghvithas and their son, had accepted the Gospel and turned to Christ. Therefore it was that when Gregory was led past them to his dungeon, they came out to seek the blessing of one soon, it seemed, destined to wear the martyr's crown. Gregory prayed with and for them, and they were all instantly restored to health. On this the youthful Athenagoṛos, who was fifteen years of age, confessed his faith in Christ and asked for baptism. Gregory received him, and directed Dasios to baptize him by the name of Theodore. This was done, and Gregory proceeded on his way, rejoicing to be counted worthy to bring one convert at least to Christ before his death.

But the work did not stop there. The youthful convert was privileged to see his mother very soon after accept the Gospel. But his father Souṛên remained immovable in his attachment to idolatry, and threatened his son with death if he did not apostatize. On this Athenagoṛos fled to a valley named Seghemnout, where he sat under a tree seven days. His father pursued him, and slew him with the sword. At night the youthful martyr's body shone with so clear a light that his sorrowing mother, who was searching for her son, saw it, and bade Dasios to inter it there. Souṛên never embraced the truth, but died in the darkness of heathenism four years later. Many years after this, the story runs, when Gregory, released from his dungeon, was going to Caesarea for consecration, the light shining from the martyr's tomb attracted his attention, and he erected a shrine there in memory of Athenagoṛos. Aghvithas lived there as an ascetic until her death seven years later. A nunnery was afterwards built upon the spot.

Encouraged by the example of the Emperor Diocletian and his coadjutors, and urged on doubtless not less by the heathen priests of his own land and by his own religious zeal, Tiridatês, almost immediately after Gregory's condemnation to death, declared war against the numerous but scattered Christians in his kingdom. For the next thirteen years, whenever his wars with the Huns and other northern tribes, and with the Persian empire, gave him leisure to turn his attention to anything besides active service in the field, the king from time to time strove with all his might to stamp out the Christian faith. During this time he published two very severe edicts against the Christians, the text of which is preserved for us by Agathangelos. In the former of these, addressed ' to the nobles, chiefs, satraps, officers of state, and to all others ' in his dominions, whether dwelling 'in towns, hamlets, villages, or in the country, to the highborn and serfs alike, Tiridatês assures them all that health and prosperity come through the favour of the gods, abundance from Aṛamazd the Noble, and provident care from the Lady Anahit. He prays that Vaḥagn the Brave may inspire them with courage, and then continues : ' When We were in the land of the Greeks, there We beheld the magnanimity of the emperors caring for the prosperity of their country, and their reverence for the altars of the gods, shown by their building temples and slaying victims, and by offering noble sacrifices of all kinds of presents and fruits from everywhere, offering all to them, and by the burning zeal of their devotions.' He points to the material blessings which the gods had showered upon the Roman empire in return. It was for this reason, he says, that the emperors compelled men to be zealous in the service of the gods, and if vulgar and ignorant persons by chance dared to interfere with or to hinder or alter the established religion of the state, the emperors would issue orders to the ruler of each several province to seize and punish such persons, so that the prosperity of the empire might increase. They inflicted the penalty of death on all who ventured to interfere with the worship of the gods.

Influenced by such august examples, ' We also,' says Tiridatês, 'have desired your prosperity and taken thought for you, so that to you also all good gifts of the gods should abound in all plentifulness, for from you they receive worship and glory, and you from them prosperity, abundance, and peace. For as every householder takes thought for his own house and family, so do We also take thought for the prosperity of the land of Armenia.'

Having then enjoined upon each and all of his subjects, gentle and simple, to honour the national gods, the king continues :—

' Wherefore, if perchance anyone be found who dishonours the gods, and they discover such a man, having bound his hands and feet and neck, let them bring him to the royal court : and his house and his possessions and his works and his property and his treasures shall all belong to him who brings forward such persons.'

Finding, as others before him had found, that such means as these were insufficient to root out the Christian faith, Tiridatês issued a second and still more severe edict. In this, after the usual greeting to his subjects, the king pointed out that, in the past history of the nation, Armenia had flourished when her people were diligent in the service of the gods, and had suffered disgrace and defeat when the contrary had been the case. He then proceeds :—

' We have especially commanded you, with reference to the heresy of the Christians (. . . since they are an unmeasured hindrance to the worship of the gods), that if any of you find any such persons, they at once bring them forward ; and that there be given from the court honours and rewards to those who denounce them. Now, if any one do not denounce such a person, but conceal him, and he be discovered, let such a man be numbered among those condemned to death, and let him be led out and die in the royal public square, and let his house be confiscated to the state. Where-fore, as I did not spare my zealous Gregory, who was dear to me, whom for this very fault I tormented very severely with exquisite tortures, and afterwards caused him to be cast into a deep *oubliette,* that he might wholly become the prey of serpents (for I did not even reckon his great services as of any account : through love and fear for the gods I esteemed them as naught), so let there be in you also this awe and fear of death. But may you live under the protection of the gods, and may you obtain favours from us also.'

Terrible as such edicts must have seemed to the unfortunate Christians then living in Armenia, we are now, in the light of history, enabled to perceive, in the very sternness and cruelty which these decrees breathe out, the last desperate struggle for life of an expiring paganism, almost hopelessly conscious that its days were numbered.

About twelve or thirteen years after Gregory had been cast into the *oubliette* to die, an event happened in Armenia which, awful as it was, finally led to the conversion of Tiridatês to the Christian faith. The story is related for us in detail by Agathangelos, and. told somewhat more briefly, is as follows :—

The Emperor Diocletian desired to obtain for him-self a beautiful damsel as a wife[1]. With this object in view, he sent messengers to various parts of the empire, with orders to find out the most beautiful maidens, and send their pictures to him, that he might choose a suitable wife for himself. The emperor's emissaries reached Rome, among other places, and there forced their way into a Christian nunnery, the abbess of which was named Gaiyanê. Among the nuns who resided there was a maiden of a pious and noble family, a foster-daughter of the abbess, famed for her exceeding beauty, and named Rhipsimê. When the emperor's messengers beheld her they were astonished and delighted, and at once painted her picture, and brought it to Diocletian, feeling con-vinced that they had discovered what they sought, the most beautiful woman in the whole Roman empire. Diocletian was so charmed with Rhipsimê's picture that he at once selected her as his consort. He fixed the time for celebrating the nuptials, and sent word to that effect to the governors of provinces and the chief men of his realm, desiring them to send the usual presents and offerings to the imperial bridegroom and bride.

When this news reached Rome, the nuns were greatly perturbed. Led by their abbess, they prayed most earnestly that their whole number might, by God's providence, be preserved, not from death or torture, but from defilement and dishonour. They then consulted together in order to decide what steps to take for their deliverance from the impending danger. It was decided that their only hope lay in flight. The whole company of holy women, therefore, leaving home and country, fled from Italy, and, after many perils and sufferings, a large number of them came to

Armenia[1]. Others are said to have taken refuge in other parts of Asia. One of them went to Georgia, where we shall hear of her again. Some were carried off as slaves, and others put to death for their faith during the persecution which was even then raging in the Roman empire. The main body, however, including Gaiyanê and Rhipsimê, on reaching Armenia, pressed on until they arrived at the city of Vagharṣhapat, where Tiridatês was then residing. Finding an old winepress in a vineyard near the city, they took up their abode in it, living as strictly in accordance with their monastic rules as they had in their nunnery in Rome. To provide themselves with daily bread they were obliged to sell in the neighbouring city any remaining articles of property they had brought with them, and finally supported themselves by the sale of glass beads, which one of their number knew how to make .

When Diocletian was informed of Rhipsimê's flight from Rome in order to escape the necessity of wedding him, his wrath and disappointment knew no bounds. It was not difficult to trace the course taken by so large a party of travellers : and hence the emperor very soon ascertained that the fugitives had succeeded in passing through Asia Minor and reaching Armenia. The latter country was under the suzerainty of the Roman empire, and the tyrant knew that Tiridatês would implicitly obey his orders. He therefore, as Agathangelos assures us , wrote a letter to the Armenian monarch, telling him of the rapid spread of Christianity in every part of the empire, and of the utter failure of all attempts to put a stop to it. He accused the Christians of worshipping the cross and 'the bones of dead men,' a reproach for which the superstitious reverence for the relics of the saints and martyrs, which had already invaded the Church, afforded only too much ground. He went on to complain of their want of reverence for the heathen gods, and of their speaking of Jesus Christ as the Creator of the universe and as God. After thus pointing out what a formidable enemy to the religion of the state Christianity had proved to be, he warned Tiridatês that a large number of nuns, led by their abbess Gaiyanê, had now entered Armenia, and would doubtless spread their faith there also, if permitted. The emperor went on to complain of Rhipsimê's flight from him, the blame of which he attributed in the main to Gaiyanê's influence. He concluded by requiring Tiridatês to search for the fugitives everywhere, and to slay them when found, unless indeed he preferred to keep for himself Rhipsimê, the most beautiful maiden in the whole of the Roman world.

On receipt of this letter, Tiridatês at once sent messengers[1] everywhere throughout the country to seek for Rhipsimê and her companions, impelled thereto partly by his desire to please the emperor his patron, and partly by the inducement held out to him in the last clause of the letter. After a most careful search had in vain been instituted towards the frontiers of Armenia, the fugitives were at last discovered in the immediate neighbourhood of the capital itself. The fame of Rhipsimê's beauty had spread far and wide, and great crowds came together to behold her. Tiridatês sent a body of soldiers to surround the place of her retreat, while he decided what should be done with her. After two days he decided to wed her, and sent some of his nobles and courtiers with royal robes to adorn her for the marriage and conduct her with all honour to the palace.

She could not be queen, for that post was already filled ; but she might, he thought, become one of his inferior wives. Suspecting this, Gaiyanê exhorted Rhipsimê to remember her vows, and not to yield to the tempta-tions of the world. In answer to the nuns' prayers a loud and fearful peal of thunder was heard, accom-panied by a voice from heaven [1] bidding Rhipsimê not to fear, but to be faithful even unto death. The steeds of the nobles who had come with the king's message, terrified by the long-continued thundering, reared and threw their riders, and then rushed madly about, trampling many of the multitude to death. When the confusion had somewhat subsided Rhipsimê gave her reply. She refused to go to court ; and the king's messengers returned to report the failure of their mission. Enraged at her refusal, Tiridatês ordered them to bring her by force, which was done. But, though all the people of the city rejoiced and sang marriage songs in honour of their king's nuptials, neither threats, persuasion, nor even violence, could induce Rhipsimê to accede to the king's desire. She forced her way out of the palace, and returned to the vineyard to her companions. Gaiyanê and two others had been taken to the palace, in order to persuade her to compliance, but had bravely ventured to encourage Rhipsimê in her determination not to yield.

A few hours after Rhipsimê's return to her retreat, she was followed by the chief executioner and his assistants, whom the enraged monarch had dispatched to execute his vengeance upon the brave Christian maiden, who was resolved to die the most terrible death rather than be false to her vows. The narrative which Agathangelos gives of the tortures inflicted on her ere at length death came to her release is too horrible to be repeated here. Her companions, to the number of thirty-two, came forward when all was over, with the pious desire to bury the mutilated remains of their sister. But the executioners assaulted them, and put them all to death with the sword, not even excepting one maiden who was ill, and could not therefore leave her retreat in the winepress, but who, when the murderers came to her, thanked God that He had not permitted her to be, through weakness of body, disappointed of the martyr s crown. The bodies were not allowed to be buried, but were cast out to be devoured by the dogs of the city and by the wild beasts. This took place on the 26th day of the Armenian month Ḥori, in the year 301. The next day Gaiyanê and her two companions were still more barbarously put to death near the southern gate of the city, not far from the bridge over the Medsamôṛ River, at the place where criminals sentenced to death were usually executed.

The king's conscience gave him no peace after the awful crime of which he had been guilty. Grief for the loss of the noble and high-souled Rhipsimê, shame at the defeat of his plans, admiration for the heroism which these Christian maidens had displayed, and the torture of remorse for his own cruelty, for six days and nights rendered sleep impossible to him. Determined at last to shake off his depression by engaging in the pleasures of the chase, he gave orders for a royal hunt, and set out with his nobles to take part in it. The royal *cortège* had not proceeded far from the

city when God's judgement fell upon Tiridatês and all his courtiers. The king himself, leaping from his chariot, became insane, his madness assuming the form of *lycanthropy,* as Nebuchadnezzar's had done many ages previously. He imagined himself a wild boar, and fled to the thickets, where he tore off his garments and associated himself with the wild beasts, rending and devouring his own flesh with his teeth. His nobles were similarly afflicted, all being possessed with evil spirits, as were many of the inhabitants of the city.
That very night a divine message came to the king's sister, *Khosṛovi*doukh*t*, to tell her the only means whereby Tiridatês could be restored to health. She was so much impressed by it that she summoned her attendants and said to them, 'A vision has appeared to me this night. A man in the form of light came and explained to me, saying, " There is no other remedy for the afflictions which have befallen you, unless you send to the city of Aṛtashat, and bring hither Gregory, who is confined there : on his coming he will teach you the medicine for the healing of your ills." On hearing this every one scoffed at the angel's message, saying that fifteen whole years had elapsed since Gregory had been cast into the dread *oubliette,* and that he must have perished very soon afterwards. When, however, the same vision was again and again repeated, a nobleman named Ôta or Ôtain was sent in haste to the fortress of Aṛtashat in order to inquire on the spot if, by any marvellous chance, Gregory still lingered on in the prison.
We must now return to Gregory, whom we left when, by Tiridatês' orders, he was cast into the *oubliette* to perish in darkness and misery. Although no previous occupant of the dungeon had ever survived to tell the tale, as their mouldering remains showed only too well, yet Gregory was kept alive by the kindness and compassion of a Christian and God-fearing widow, who dwelt in the castle under which he was confined.
Warned by a heavenly messenger, this woman baked a small cake every day, and let it down into the dungeon. This she continued to do regularly during the whole term of his imprisonment.
When Ôta reached Aṛtashat, he immediately hastened to the dungeon to see whether it were possible that Gregory still survived. He let down a rope, and called out Gregory's name, directing him, if still living, to seize the rope, that he might be drawn up. This Gregory did ; and thus at last, after between thirteen and fifteen years of solitary confinement in his loathsome dungeon, was once more permitted to see the light of day. He was as one raised from the dead in order to accomplish the task to which God had called him. Worn by long privations and want of food and clothes, his body, we are told, when he emerged from the *oubliette,* was as black as a coal. When he learnt what had befallen the king, and heard the reason of his release, Gregory, waiting only for clothing, started with Ôta for the capital. When he drew near to Vagharṣhapat, the first person he met was King Tiridatês himself, naked and possessed by the devil, rending his own flesh with his teeth in his frenzy and foaming at the mouth like a furious wild beast. A little later the nobles were met with in a similar awful condition of mind and body. Dismounting from his chariot, Gregory knelt down on the ground and prayed to God to have mercy on them and forgive their sins. They were immediately restored to their senses, and, falling at Gregory's feet, implored his forgiveness for the cruel treatment he had received at their hands. He replied, ' I am but a mortal man like yourselves. Kneel not to me, but fall low in the dust before God, the Creator of all things, for against Him have ye sinned ; and He will perfectly heal and forgive you.'
Gregory then clothed them, and proceeded to inquire where the bodies of the martyred virgins lay. Full of shame and remorse, the king and his courtiers led him to the spot where Rhipsimê and her companions had suffered for their faith. Although nine days had now passed since their martyrdom, the mutilated remains had been divinely preserved safe from corruption. Gregory reverently collected them for burial, clothing them in the rent and tattered garments they had worn. The nobles brought the most costly robes to wrap them in, but Gregory refused to permit them to be contaminated by the touch of the garments of the heathen Gregory then caused three martyr memorial shrines to be built as tombs for the martyred nuns : one where Gaiyanê and her two companions had suffered, near the bridge over the Medsamôṛ, another on the spot consecrated by the death of Rhipsimê and her companions, and the third in the vineyard where they had dwelt, and where he himself resided during the erection of these buildings. The king and his nobles gladly and readily set to work to dig the graves, while their wives and daughters, headed by Queen Ashmen and Princess *Khosṛovi*doukh*t*, collected in their aprons the excavated soil and carried it out of the pits. During this time the king and his courtiers were clothed in sackcloth and sat in ashes, to show their deep penitence. Gregory, at their earnest request, devoted more than sixty days continuously to instructing them in the Christian faith, ' striving like a wise physician,' as Agathangelos informs us, 'to discover the remedy suitable ' for the cure of their diseased souls. The spirit in which he laboured is well expressed by the words which that author ascribes to him : ' Every day there in the deep dungeon,' he said to them, ' I with open eyes beheld the angel of God, who always encouraged me : and just so now too I see him, and he says to me, " Be of good cheer, stand firm ; for the Lord God hath preserved thee, and hath deemed thee worthy of His service, and hath assigned to thee the labour of His husbandry, that thou also, having entered in with the other labourers, mightest receive as thy hire the imperishable reward of Christ." '
Such seems to be, in as concise and simple a form as possible, the true narrative of the conversion of Tiridatês and the leading nobles of Armenia. Owing doubtless to the very extensive interpolations (chiefly in the interest of Rome) that have crept into our present text, the printed work of Agathangelos abounds in marvels not only incredible, but ludicrous, and which exactly resemble many of the mediaeval legends of the saints. For example, we are there told that the king and his nobles were actually transformed, as by some Circean enchantment, into veritable wild boars of enormous size and savage aspect. On their repentance, and at Gregory's prayer for them when he first met them, although the devils were driven out and their minds were restored to sanity, so as to enable them to profit by his preaching, yet they still retained their bestial form, though able to speak to him. Only somewhat later were their hoofs

again changed into hands and feet, in order to permit them to use pickaxe and spade, and so to dig the virgin martyrs' graves. Tiridatês also, we are informed, employed his gigantic strength to good purpose by ascending to the summit of Mount Masis (Ararat) and carrying[1] down thence enormous stones, to help forward the building of the shrines. All this points to the free use of the imagination at a date much later than that of the original Agathangelos. On the other hand , Moses of *Khoṛenê* speaks of Agathangelos' work as extant in his own time and thoroughly reliable, though he gives no indication that it then contained such marvels as are found in the work which now bears that author's name. Zenobius, a contemporary of Agathangelos, speaks of his history as then well known, and later Armenian historians unanimously assert the same. As Agathangelos himself informs us in the preface to his history, he was a Roman by birth, and accompanied Tiridatês to Armenia as his private secretary. He wrote his history by the express command of Tiridatês himself, who thought it well that the marvellous circumstances which finally brought about the conversion of Armenia should be handed down in writing for the information of posterity. Agathangelos tells us that he himself was well acquainted with both Greek and Latin. In what tongue he composed his history is a matter of dispute ; but, as the present Armenian alphabet had not then been invented, and as he was a foreigner, it can hardly have been in that language. The probability is that he composed his work in Greek. The present Armenian text is a translation into that tongue made in the fifth century of our era, and undoubtedly from a *Syriac* version of the original work. It is most unfortunate that so many interpolations should have been allowed to creep into the text ; but the general accuracy of the narrative is completely confirmed by Zenobius and Moses of Khoṛenê, the latter of whom gives virtually the same account of Gregory's work, though in a very brief epitome. It remains only to add that the *present* Greek text of Agathangelos is certainly not the original, but is merely a comparatively late version from our present Armenian text, with slight modifications here and there, and the retention of a few chapters at the beginning, to which Moses of *Khoṛenê* refers, but which are not found in the present Armenian version.

CHAPTER VIII

TRIUMPH OF CHRISTIANITY IN ARMENIA

'Hairaṛatean gavarin, i thagavoṛanist kayeansn, bgh*kh*etsin Ḥayots tann Thoṛgomah shnoṛḥkh khaṛozouthean avetaṛanin patouiṛanatsn Astoudson.'—Agathangelos, *Patm.* kl. 107.

' From the canton of Airaṛat, the station where the kings abode, welled forth for the Armenians of the house of Togarmah the grace of the preaching of the Gospel of the commandments of God.'

THE spiritual conquest of Armenia, begun so many generations previously, and for which so many martyrs had died and so many noble men and women had toiled and suffered during nearly three centuries, was now nearing its completion. The leaven of truth had, as we have already seen, long been working ; and many in all parts of the country already believed in Christ as the Saviour of the World. The news of the coming of Rhipsimê and her devoted companions had been noised abroad by the king's determined search for them ; and the awful narrative of their martyrdom must have struck horror into many hearts, mingled with wonder and admiration for the virgin martyrs who had been found faithful even unto death. While Christians doubtless felt nerved by the news of their courage and devotion to undertake more boldly fresh efforts for the spread of that glorious Gospel which had told them that Christ had ' abolished death and brought life and immortality to light,' many even of the earnest heathen must have realized that no amount of persecution could ever succeed in crushing the Christian faith, and must have been drawn towards the religion which produced such noble lives and such heroic deaths. The tidings of the terrible punishment that had fallen upon the persecuting king and his nobles, and the news of Gregory's wonderful preservation and almost resurrection from the dead to preach the Gospel to the people of Armenia, would still further prepare men's hearts to receive the divine message of salvation thus wonderfully brought to them. Death is always an object of terror to the natural man ; and in heathen Armenia it was, as we have seen, rendered no less gloomy and terrible by the weeping and wailing which showed to how little hope or comfort the survivors could cling. The heathen from their own experience knew well how they and their fathers had been ' all their lifetime subject to bondage ' through fear of death. They had with their own eyes seen that death, even in its most cruel form, had no terrors for Christ's true followers, and would have confessed the truth of the words in which Athanashis, Bishop of Alexandria, only a few years later, celebrates the Christians' delivery from the dread of the last enemy. We cannot resist the temptation to introduce the passage here.

' Before men believe in Christ,' says Athanasius , 'they regard Death as terrible, and dread him. But when they pass over into His faith and doctrine, so greatly do they despise Death that they even rush willingly to encounter him, and become witnesses to the resurrection won from him by the Saviour. For even those who are of tender age are zealous to die, and not only men but even women by their austerities plot against him. So feeble has he grown that even those women who were formerly deluded by him now mock him as himself dead and gone. For, just as when a tyrant has been overcome in war by a rightful king, and has been bound hand and foot, all who go by scoff at him, striking and reproaching him, no longer dreading his fury and cruelty because of their victorious king ; so also when Death has been overcome and held up to public scorn by the Saviour on the cross, and bound hand and foot, all they that pass by in Christ tread him down, and, bearing witness to Christ, scoff at Death, taunting him and repeating what has been pronounced against him from above, " O Death, where is thy sting ? O Grave, where is thy victory ? " '

When Gregory had completed the teaching and instruction in the Christian faith which he gave Tiridatês and his courtiers, he prayed for their complete restoration to bodily health and strength. The prayer was heard, and all of them who had been smitten with leprosy, palsy, dropsy, or some other disease for their sins, were instantly made whole. A vision of the Saviour Himself was vouchsafed to Gregory at the spot where these miracles of healing were wrought, in the neighbourhood of Vagharṣhapat ; and the church built there is regarded as the mother church of Armenia to the present day, and the place is still called Êjmiadsin ('the Descent of the Only Begotten '), from the circumstance of the manifestation of Christ which is believed there to have cheered and strengthened the Apostle of Armenia for the arduous labours that still awaited him.

The new converts, filled with love and zeal, were ready to go forth and preach the faith throughout the length and breadth of their fatherland. Tiridatês, the former persecutor of Christ's followers, longed now, like another St. Paul, to proclaim the Gospel of Christ which he had once scoffed at. He called a council of his nobles and greater barons at Vagharṣhapat, therefore, shortly after his recovery, to consider what steps should be taken to remove the abominations of idolatry from the whole land, to 'cast out the stumbling-blocks,' as Agathangelos says, and to bring the nation at large to the foot of the Cross. By general consent it was resolved to entrust this task to Gregory, and the king and his nobles promised to support and assist him in it in every possible way. As a proof of his sincerity in the work, the king desired Gregory to begin by shattering the idols belonging to the palace, which had for generations been worshipped by his ancestors and himself. This having been done, by the command of Tiridatês Gregory started from Vagharṣhapat with the object of destroying all the idols and idol temples in the province of Aiṛaṛat and ultimately in the whole of Armenia, the king accompanying him with an army. As yet Gregory had not been ordained, so he did not feel at liberty to baptize his converts or to consecrate churches, though authorized by the king to erect the latter everywhere on the ruins of the idol temples which he destroyed.

The first place to which the royal party directed their march was the city of Aṛtashat itself, where Gregory had so long suffered for the faith once for all delivered to the saints. There all the heathen temples were razed to the ground and the idols destroyed. At the town of Eṛazmoin there was a celebrated shrine sacred to Tiuṛ, the ' scribe of the gods,' the interpreter of dreams and visions and the author of all theology. When this temple was destroyed, we are told, the gods, fearing that their cause was forever lost in Armenia, wailed and lamented bitterly, crying aloud, 'Alas for us! for Christ the Son of Mary, daughter of men, has put us to flight and expelled us from the whole earth. Here, too, it has befallen us to be obliged to flee by means of those who were dead and those who were bound. But whither shall *we* flee ? for His glory hath filled the whole world. Let us go to the inhabitants of the Caucasus Mountains in the northern quarters ; perhaps some device may be found, and we may live V Those who heard this lament of the defeated gods were thereby confirmed in their belief in the victorious Christian faith. All the treasures found in Tiuṛ's temple were given to be distributed among the poor and infirm. The landed estates attached to the temple, and hitherto owned by the priests, were set aside for the service of the Church. This process, with some trifling variety, was continued, until in every city, town, village and hamlet in Armenia a place had been assigned for the erection of the house of God, generally on the site of a ruined heathen temple. Agathangelos tells us that Gregory ' raised no altars there,' as he had not yet been ordained ' priest ' ; but instead of this he everywhere erected crosses, as emblems of the Christian faith, and the ignorant converts transferred their adoration from their old to these new idols. Unfortunately, however, neither Gregory nor his chronicler seems to have perceived that a Christian idol was no nobler and more legitimate an object of worship than a heathen one.

Wherever the reforming march of the king and Gregory led them, the former vied with the latter in preaching the Gospel and teaching the new converts, who came forward in large numbers for instruction. They advanced into the canton of Daṛanaghikh and reached the village of Thoṛdan, where there stood the temple of ' the resplendent goddess Baṛshimnia.' This they destroyed, and divided its treasures among the poor, erecting the cross among the ruins. They next advanced to the ancient and renowned fortress of Ani, the burial-place of the Kings of Armenia. There stood the far-famed temple of Aṛamazd, father of all the gods, which now shared the fate of all other heathen shrines. Marching thence into the canton of Ekeghikh, the warriors of the Cross reached the sacred town of Eṛêz, where in bygone days Gregory had witnessed the fervour of Tiridatês' devotion to the goddess Anahit, and had himself suffered the most fearful tortures rather than do sacrifice to her. Here, we are told, the gods made a fierce stand, and ' fought like shield-bearing warriors ' ; but were routed. Tiridatês assisted Gregory in breaking in pieces the golden image of Anahit, as also that of her sister Nanê, which stood near the bank of the river Gail, in the town of Thil. The treasures of both temples were on this occasion reserved for the service of the Church.

Wherever the good seed was sown during this missionary journey, men came forward readily and heartily to receive it. Testimony was borne to the truth of Gregory's teaching by the miracles which (it is reported) were wrought by him through Divine grace. The king preached publicly, confessing his sins and telling how God had shown mercy on him and his courtiers, forgiving them their sins, and giving them the light of His glorious Gospel. The last place mentioned as having been visited on this occasion by Gregory and the king was the canton of Deṛjan. There, in a village named

Bagayaṛichn, stood a renowned temple of Mihr. This was demolished. The king reserved the site of the temple for that of a future church, but divided among the poor the not inconsiderable treasures found in the temple.
It now became apparent that the time had fully come for the baptism of the numerous converts who wished to profess the Christian faith. It was necessary also to take steps towards establishing Christianity as the national religion of the country, and to make arrangements for public worship and the ecclesiastical government of the Church of Armenia. Tiridatês, his queen Ashmen, and his sister, Princess *Khosṛov*idou*kh*t, Gregory's three most distinguished and most zealous converts, after due deliberation among themselves, resolved to call together a great national council at the capital, Vagharṣhapat, and there to decide what should be done in order to accomplish the work which had been so zealously begun. The king therefore marched his army back to Vagharṣhapat. Soon after he summoned to meet him the chief nobles, governors of provinces, judges, generals of the army and other dignitaries. When they had assembled, the king explained to them the important nature of the business about which they had met to deliberate. After detailing briefly the circumstances which had led to his own conversion and that of a very large portion of the population of the country, Tiridatês pointed out the fact that, in accordance with the command of Christ Himself, it was necessary that they should be admitted into the communion of the Christian Church by means of baptism. Arrangements must also be made for the further instruction and training of the converts, and for the further propagation of the Gospel throughout the whole land. This being the case, it was desirable to establish a Christian hierarchy in the stead of that which was now being put down. He therefore called upon the council to nominate a man fitted to rule and arrange the affairs of the nascent Armenian Church, who should be consecrated bishop or archbishop of the whole land. Tiridatês concluded by declaring his conviction that, in the person of Gregory, God Most High had given them a spiritual pastor, and one in every way worthy of the high office to which God in His marvellous providence had so clearly called him. The whole assembly approved of this recommendation, and Gregory was chosen to receive ordination as chief pastor of the whole Church of Armenia.
Here, however, a great difficulty, and one which for a time seemed insuperable, presented itself. Gregory's modesty made him shrink from accepting the honour offered to him by the representatives of the whole kingdom. He was a layman, he said, and felt himself unworthy to be ordained to the holy office of the priesthood, ' unworthy to mediate between God and man.' For a time nothing sufficed to move him from this decision. But at last, as Agathangelos assures us, a wondrous vision appeared to King Tiridatês. An angel from heaven revealed himself to him, and declared that God had sent him to tell the king His will. Your duty V he said,' is to procure for Gregory without delay ordination to the priesthood, in order that he may illuminate you all with baptism.' At the same time a similar vision was vouchsafed to Gregory himself, commanding him to submit, and no longer to resist God's will in the matter. As he now clearly perceived that he was divinely called to the office of bishop, Gregory yielded to the unanimous desire of the representatives of his adopted country.
Tiridatês thereupon chose sixteen of the leading nobles and officers of the army to accompany Gregory to Caesarea in Cappadocia, whither he decided to send him for ordination and consecration. He wrote a letter, in his own name and in that of the queen and the Princess *Khosṛov*idou*kh*t, to Leontius, Archbishop of Caesarea, setting forth the events which had recently occurred in Armenia, and desiring him to consecrate Gregory as ' high priest[1] ' of the country, and to appoint him to the office of 'shepherd and physician ' of the Armenian nation. The king's messengers took with them most munificent gifts, such as offerings of gold and silver, together with horses, mules, garments of different kinds, and ornaments for the churches of Caesarea. Gregory, in a royal chariot, richly decorated with gold and drawn by white mules, accompanied them. A large body of troops also attended the bishop-elect on his journey. On their arrival at Caesarea they presented to Leontius the letter Tiridatês had sent. Leontius, on reading it, received Gregory with much honour, and assembled a large number of the bishops of Cappadocia to assist in the consecration of the first Archbishop of Armenia, which was duly (A. D. 302) celebrated with much rejoicing on the part of the Christians resident in that part of the Roman empire, who, amid their persecutions, thanked God that one other land had gladly received the Gospel of His love.
Almost immediately after his consecration, Gregory returned to Armenia, bringing with him (in the royal chariot drawn by white mules, which he had vacated in their favour) the most valuable gifts which, in the estimation of too many of the Christians of that period, he could possibly have received, viz. the relics of John the Baptist and of another martyr called Athanaginês (Athênogenês ?). When he reached the canton of Taṛôn, he learned that it contained three great heathen temples, full of gold and silver and other valuable gifts given by former Kings of Armenia. These temples were sacred to three of the most popular deities of heathen Armenia—to Vaḥagn, ' the player with dragons,' the Hercules of Armenian mythology ; to the ' Golden Mother,' Anaḥit ; and to Astghik or Aphroditê respectively. They were situated near Mount Khaṛkhê, on the bank of the river Euphrates. Gregory decided to destroy these temples and put an end to the sacrifices which the heathen inhabitants still continued to offer to these deities. Accordingly he advanced towards the place where they stood. On the way the white mules which drew the chariot containing the holy relics came to a halt in a certain little mountain glade, and resolutely refused to budge a step from the place where they stood. While Gregory and his companions wondered at this, an angel appeared to him, and told him to build on that very spot a martyr memorial in honour of the two saints whose bones he had brought to Armenia with him. This was at once begun, and soon completed.
Meanwhile, according to Agathangelos[1], the soldiers in Gregory's train had gone forward and reached the three shrines, which, however, they in vain attempted to enter. The magical power of the heathen priests prevented them

from finding any way of gaining an entrance ; and they were obliged to return and tell Gregory of their non-success. On hearing this, Gregory, cross in hand, advanced towards the three temples. At his request, a violent wind, blowing from the cross itself, arose and completely blew away the temples, with their attendant priests and their hoarded treasures. The annihilation of these heathen shrines was so utter that not a single trace remained to show that such buildings had ever stood there. As a natural result, many of the heathen, seeing the helplessness of their false gods, asked for baptism. Gregory remained there for some time, preaching the Gospel to them and preparing them for that holy rite. He laid the foundation there of the first properly consecrated church in the whole country.

We must here observe that Zenobius, a Syrian clergyman who accompanied Gregory on this expedition, and wrote a narrative of it which is still preserved, gives us a totally different account of (apparently) this very event. He names precisely the same spot, but tells us that, instead of the temples of the Armenian deities we have mentioned above, there were in that place shrines dedicated to the worship of Demetrius and Sisianê. These were, we are informed, two Indian princes, who, driven from their native land, came to Armenia in the days of King Vagharṣhak, and were by him assigned the canton of Taṛôn as their residence. Fifteen years later, Vagharṣhak, finding them guilty of some offence, put them both to death, but appointed their sons rulers of that canton. These latter made huge brazen images of their fathers, and worshipped them in Mount Khaṛkhê. When news reached the temple that Gregory was advancing upon it with the intention of razing it to the ground, the chief priest Aṛtzan and his son Demetrius, with a body of armed priests, laid wait for him in an ambush upon the top of the hill. When Gregory and his companions, fearing no repulse, drew near, the heathen priests fell upon them unawares and hurled them down the hill. Gregory's followers, astonished at this quite unexpected resistance, compelled him to take refuge in the neighbouring fortress of Oghkan. But in the previous struggle the chief priest Aṛtzan had been slain by a chief of the family of Angegh. Demetrius succeeded him in the chieftainship, and collected all the available soldiers of the country to fight against Gregory. He thus mustered a force of about 7,000 troops, and fought bravely, but in the ensuing battle he was slain and his forces scattered. This is the only occasion recorded, during all Gregory's evangelistic and iconoclastic tours, on which the heathen priests ventured to fight for their faith.

At the place where he had begun to build the first consecrated Christian church in Armenia, Gregory decided to administer baptism to some of the many converts whom he had prepared for the sacred rite. He first baptized the sixteen nobles who had accompanied him to Caesarea, and who were still in his train, and then proceeded to administer baptism to all others whom he judged fit to receive it, ending with local converts. Agathangelos says that during twenty days more than one hundred and ninety thousand persons received baptism there, from Gregory himself and from the other clergy who had accompanied him on his return from Cappadocia. Gregory also erected an 'altar' and administered Holy Communion there to his converts. He ordained that a yearly festival should be observed at the martyr-shrine he had erected on the seventh of the month Saḥmi. Gregory then proceeded to ordain priests and deacons, some of whom he put in charge of the new church and the local converts, and he took the rest with him, intending to appoint them to the cure of souls in the various towns and villages throughout the country where he should find numerous converts. He then continued his journey, endeavouring to visit every city and village in the country. Wherever the people seemed inclined to accept Christianity, Gregory built a church and baptized those who seemed to have believed with an intelligent faith.

Hearing of Gregory's return to Armenia, King Tiridatês, accompanied by Queen Ashkhên and Princess *Khosṛov*idou*kh*t, set out from the capital to meet and welcome him. The royal party, on reaching the town of Bagavan, halted there for a month to await the arrival of the archbishop. Gregory, accompanied by a great host of people, at length drew near to the foot of Mount Niphatês. The king met him on the bank of the Euphrates, and returned with him to Bagavan. There the envoys who accompanied Gregory presented to the king the letter which Leontius had written in reply to the king's epistle which he had sent, requesting that Gregory should be consecrated.

Gregory remained at Bagavan for a whole month, during which time he preached and taught, and prayed every day with great zeal and devotion. The king and his whole court obeyed his commands as if they were ' those of an angel of God.' During this time Gregory founded a church in the town, and deposited some of the remaining relics there. But his chief care was devoted to preparing the members of the royal family and the soldiers of the army to receive Christian baptism. When, after a month's careful preparation, he thought that they were fit for it, one morning he descended with the king and queen and Princess *Khosṛov*idou*kh*t and the other catechumens to the bank of the river Euphrates, and there baptized them in the river, in the name of the Father, and of the Son, and of the Holy Ghost. It is said that Tiridatês, at his baptism, took the name of John. Tiridatês—if we except the case of Abgar on the ground of insufficient evidence—was not only the first King of Armenia who received baptism, but perhaps the first known sovereign of any country thus to range himself under the banner of the Cross. His baptism took place in A.D. 302. It required a considerable degree of courage and faith for Tiridatês to take this step ; for not only were many of his own people very far from really welcoming the downfall of heathenism and the establishment of Christianity in the country, but the enmity of two great neighbouring states, the Byzantine and the Persian empires, both at that time ruled by monarchs strongly hostile to the religion of the Cross, was certain to be aroused thereby, and might readily lead to misfortune, and even to the total overthrow of his dynasty. We shall see that at a later date Tiridatês was called upon to undergo much suffering from these various quarters. But, trusting in the Saviour, whose voice had found an echo in his heart, Tiridatês confessed Christ the crucified in baptism, resolved to risk the loss of all things for His sake. According to Agathangelos (who seems to have been thoroughly imbued with the superstitions of his age), the important event of the king's baptism was marked by a miraculous token of Divine approval. When the royal converts were stepping down into the waters of the river, ' a wondrous sign appeared front God. For the waters of the river, ceasing to flow, turned back from that place : and a mighty light was manifest, in the likeness of a shining pillar, and this stood above the waters of the stream. Above it was the likeness of the cross of the Lord. It shone so brightly that it dimmed the rays of the sun. And the anointing oil, which Gregory was pouring upon the people, circling around in the midst of the river, played round about[1] ' those who were receiving baptism. This marvellous vision was visible for three days, and then vanished. During that time no fewer than 150,000 of the royal troops are stated to have been baptized in the waters of the Euphrates. The baptisms were celebrated with great rejoicings, the catechumens coming to the rite clad in white garments, bearing burning torches in their hands, and singing psalms as they marched.

During the ensuing week we are told that more than four millions (!!!) of people, men, women and children, received baptism from Gregory and his assistants . It is needless to point out the absurdity of the exaggeration contained in such a statement. The fact seems to be that (as occurred in Russia when Vladimir, the first Christian prince of that country, received baptism) great numbers of the nobles and of the common people followed the example of their sovereign, doubtless believing that he was wiser than themselves, and more likely to have found out that Truth for which so many, in all ages, have professed to long, and so few are ready to seek with all their hearts .

Bagavan being a holy city in heathen times (as its name—the city of the god or the gods—denotes), there was a great annual festival held there on the Armenian New Year's Day, in honour of Amanoṛ and Vanatouṛ, two of the minor deities of the land. Knowing with how much tenacity people cling to such ancient observances, and despairing of entirely putting a stop to such a festival, Gregory determined to order its retention, while at the same time associating it no longer with heathen but with Christian ideas. He therefore transferred to John the Baptist and Athanaginês, who were to his mind destined to be the patron saints of Armenia, the honour previously paid on that festival to the above-named heathen deities. This is only one instance of what was part of Gregory's unchanging policy in such matters ; but about this we shall have more to say elsewhere.

After this, Gregory resumed his itinerating work among the people of the country at large. Nothing could exceed the zeal and devotion which characterized the ' Illuminator' in this work. He travelled through the whole land, visiting, either in person or by deputy, every city, town, village and hamlet in all the provinces and cantons of Armenia. His journeys and evangelistic tours extended from the confines of Syria to the ' Gates of the Alans ' in the Caucasus, from Nisibis to the Caspian Sea, from Cappadocia to Atropatenê (Âzarbâijân), and to the utmost limits of Armenia. Of course the whole population of the country did not at once become Christian, for we learn of one sect or body of sun-worshippers, styled Aṛevoṛdikh, or ' Sons of the Sun,' who lingered on until the time of the celebrated Neṛsês Shnoṛhali, in some villages bordering on Mesopotamia. Nor were all who received baptism true believers, as after events showed very plainly. Yet Gregory spared no effort, and grudged no amount of toil and exertion, in order to leave no one in the country without a knowledge of the Gospel of Christ. At his request Tiridatês issued edicts appointing suitable places in each canton for the people to assemble at stated times for instruction in the doctrines of the faith. There Gregory himself, or the preachers appointed by him for the purpose, proclaimed the Gospel message to rich and poor, noble and serf, old and young alike. In order to have a sufficient number of labourers for this purpose, it was, in the first instance, necessary to have recourse to aid from without. After his consecration, on his return to Armenia, he brought with him a number of bishops, abbots, monks and ordinary clergy, to aid him in his great work in the Lord's harvest field. Of these, in a letter to Leontius, Archbishop of Caesarea, Gregory himself says, ' Those whom thou hast given to me I account as precious pearls.' A noble testimony this, from such a man as Gregory, to the zeal and devotion of his fellow-labourers. But as the work grew and prospered he found himself compelled to appeal once more to Leontius for still more missionaries. Writing, therefore, to the Archbishop of Caesarea, he says, ' Because of the familiar affection which thou entertainest for me, I entreat thee to bestow upon me yet another gift . . . i. e. that thou wouldest thrust forth labourers into this harvest. Among whom, one of the good labourers whom I entreat of thee is Eliazar, Bishop of Nistria, who is brother of Zenobius, the bishop whom, when he was brought to me, I consecrated to the land of the Mamikonians. Now do thou send him also along with other labourers and ministers. Especially do thou send Timotheus, Bishop of the Adonians, whom also thou didst praise for his acquaintance with the Scriptures, a thing very necessary for this country.'

The patriarch acceded to Gregory's request for more men, and sent a large reinforcement to aid Gregory in his work. In his letter in reply to the one we have just quoted, Leontius says, ' I consent that Epiphanius, a disciple of Antonius, should come to thee, bringing with him forty ascetic men clothed in sackcloth, pure in their morals, who have renounced the world. When thou hast received them, do thou appoint Epiphanius abbot of that monastery of thine where Zenobius is.' Thus for a time Gregory was supplied with a number of earnest and zealous coadjutors, all of whom, however, were foreigners, mostly Syrians.

Gregory was too wise and too devoted a man to be content to let the future of the Church of Christ in Armenia depend upon the efforts of foreign clergy, probably entirely ignorant of Armenian, and not in every instance able to gain the confidence and affec-tion of such a nation as that which they had come to evangelize. He saw the absolute necessity of raising up a body of able and zealous native clergy as soon as possible, and training them to carry on the work which he had been privileged to begin. We are informed by Agathangelos that he therefore ordained to the ministry such of the idol-priests as, after conversion and baptism, seemed suitable. This, of course, was not in every case a wise step to take, but it had some obvious advantages. In the first place, they were already the recognized religious leaders of the people. Again, they were doubtless the best educated men, as a class, of which Armenia could at that time boast, as anything resembling indigenous literature was entirely in their hands. Once more, it was politic to gain over to his side the influence of the old priesthood, instead of driving the whole body into determined opposition to himself and the faith which he preached. The disadvantages of the plan are clear to us, and must have been equally so to Gregory. Whether they are outweighed by the advantages detailed above may well be considered doubtful.

A far wiser policy was to establish schools for the education of the youth of the country and their training in the Christian faith. This was done by Tiridatês at Gregory's request. The greatest care was taken to obtain good and faithful teachers ; and these seem to have been paid out of the state funds. The result was that the wild and hitherto almost absolutely unlettered people of Armenia were soon noted for their knowledge of the Word of God, even although as yet there was no really suitable alphabet employed in writing Armenian, and no portion of the Bible had as yet been translated into the language of the country. Especial attention was devoted to the education of the sons of the converted heathen priests, whose children, like those of the Brâhmans in India, might naturally be presumed to have a special aptitude for the acquisition of learning. These were assembled in separate classes and taught. They were divided into two sections, one of which was taught the Syriac language and literature, and the other the Greek. Both Syriac and Greek were already to some extent understood in Armenia. The king, having been brought up in the Roman empire, had carefully studied the Greek language. Many of the nobility and some of the merchants were doubtless acquainted with Greek, at least to some extent. But there is good reason to believe that—owing partly to commerce and partly to the fact that almost all Christian influences brought to bear upon Armenia for centuries before Gregory's time were Syrian—the Syriac language was far more widely known by the mass of the people than was Greek. Many of the clergy sent to Gregory from Cappadocia were Syrians ; and it is stated by Armenian historians that, in public worship and teaching, the Scriptures were for a long time read in Syriac and then translated orally into Armenian. This, we know, was very much what took place in the Christian Church in Persia, where almost all Christian influences were of Syrian origin. All early translations into Armenian (including that of Agathangelos himself) seem to have been made, not from Greek, but from Syrian, even when the original work was Greek. Gradually, however, the knowledge of Syriac in Armenia died out, its place being in some measure taken by Greek. But even to the present day not a few of the religious and even some of the civil terms used in Armenian are distinctly of Syriac origin. We need merely instance *khaḥanah,* a priest, and *thag,* a crown, to illustrate this.

Very naturally Gregory made the capital, Vagharṣhapat, his starting-point in carrying out his plans for the evangelization of the country. He built a church there on the site previously fixed. In visiting the provinces he gave orders that churches should be erected on the site of the ruined heathen shrines. He appointed clergy to minister there, and consecrated bishops to superintend the affairs of each dis-trict. Agathangelos gives a list of no less than twelve bishops who were all the sons of heathen priests . Many of them Gregory had himself adopted and brought up with spiritual care in the fear of God, as if they were his own children. One of them was Albianus or Albinus, whom Gregory appointed Bishop of Ḥarkh, near the Euphrates. Another (apparently) of the same name was put in charge of the court and royal troops. The latter is described as ' a true and godly man.' as no doubt many others also were. In all, Gregory is said to have consecrated more than 400 bishops, besides a great multitude of presbyters and deacons.

Gregory did not confine his efforts to merely preaching the Gospel, but strove to lead the people to obey it in their lives. And, not content with setting them a noble example by his own blameless life, he endeavoured to put down injustice and tyranny wherever possible. His own personal character, the piety and earnestness which marked his whole conduct, and his immense influence at court and among the people, enabled him to bring pressure to bear upon the oppressor and to relieve the "oppressed. He compelled many an unjust creditor to permit the papers upon which his claim was based to be torn up. He delivered captives and prisoners from the hands of the captors, ' snatching them away by the terror and might of the glory of God.' During all the days of his life he bore the Saviour's name before kings and princes, and all adversaries of the faith. None were too humble and none too vile for him to endeavour to bring to them the light of life and the good news of salvation through Christ. He made Armenia his fatherland ; and the fact that, though a Parthian by descent, he had been born in their country, had married an Armenian wife, and spoke their lan-guage fluently, doubtless aided him in accomplishing a work and establishing an influence in Armenia which no one else in all history has ever been able to claim.

It was not until he had done all this, and laid well and truly a broad foundation for the rising Church of Armenia, that Gregory thought himself justified in retiring from what he deemed a worldly life to the more congenial solitude of what was then considered to be the higher and more spiritual life of a recluse. Taking Elijah and John the Baptist for his models, instead of the higher examples set by the apostles and by the Saviour Himself, Gregory began from time to time to retire to the solitude of the mountains, and there live on herbs and devote himself to watchings and fastings and to reading religious books. These retreats gradually became more and more frequent and of longer continuance. Although he used to come down from the mountains whenever it seemed necessary to do so, whether to instruct his disciples or to help in settling the affairs of the Church or the nation, or to intervene when any unexpected occurrence rendered his presence and counsel desirable, yet his frequent absence from the court and seclusion from the world became more and more a serious inconvenience as time went on. We can well understand an earnest, thoughtful and pious man like Gregory, seeing the vanity of worldly things, and wishing to have more leisure for spiritual meditation and study of God's Word, retiring from the distractions of the court and devoting himself to purely religious work. At court this was impossible, for the king and the whole of the rulers of the nation depended upon him for guidance and direction in all matters of conduct. For a man like Gregory, luxury and even comfort had no charms. Ambition might naturally exercise a great influence over such a mind ; but in Gregory's case devotion to his Divine Master's cause must have cast out all self-love. There was much, therefore, that must have led Gregory to yearn for the quiet and seclusion of a recluse, though his love for the Armenian people made him unceasing in his itineration and preaching of the Gospel. But the ideas of the age in which he lived must also have had their influence upon him, Christians had then begun to believe that to retire to the desert, and there to macerate oneself with fastings, watchings and scourgings, was to live an ' angelic life,' and was the best way to please God. Such a life must originally have been forced upon many an earnest Christian when, fleeing from persecution, he found the wild beasts of the wilderness more merciful than his fellow-men, and the stony floor of a mountain cave a softer couch than the rack from which he had escaped. We can well understand, therefore, how Christians gradually grew, through their reverence for these men, ' of whom the world was not worthy,' to believe that their method of life was particularly holy and pleasing to God. The introduction of monkery also owed much to the example of Indian ascetics, Brâhmans and Buddhists, the fame of whose austerities had spread far and wide. Thus a method of life for which neither the Old nor the New Testament gives any authorization (except in the case of *absolute necessity,* as in those of Elijah, the Maccabean martyrs mentioned in the eleventh chapter of the Epistle to the Hebrews, and perhaps John the Baptist) gradu-ally came to be regarded as ' the religious life,' and as especially blessed. Agathangelos falls into this error in speaking of Gregory's retirement; but we may perhaps hope that the 'Illuminator ' himself held more scriptural views on the subject, and that he in his latter years adopted the life of a hermit because he found that in this way he was able to do actually more work for God and his adopted country than he could have done by living amid the distrac-tions of Tiridatês' court and camp.

The establishment of Christianity as the national religion of Armenia produced a temporary breach of the friendly relations which had subsisted between Armenia and the Roman empire ever since Diocletian had restored Tiridatês to the throne of his fathers. Galerius was now Emperor of the East, and had long hated and persecuted the Christians throughout his dominions. He had committed the sovereignty of Syria, Palestine and Egypt to his creature Maximin ; and the latter was inclined by his own cruelty of disposition and hatred of the purity inculcated by Christianity to carry out to the full the persecuting edicts of the emperor. Eusebius gives a terrible account of the fearful sufferings which this monster in human form inflicted upon the followers of Christ in every province over which he held sway. Not content with this, Maximin, excited apparently by the tidings of the triumphs of the Cross in Armenia, made war upon Tiridatês, and marched an army into that country. The date of this expedition cannot be precisely fixed, as different authorities place it at A.D. 308, 311, and 315, but the earliest of the three dates seems the most probable. Eusebius speaks of the Armenians as having been from ancient times the friends and allies of the Romans, and praises their piety and zeal for the Christian faith, which was already known to have become the established religion of the country. The tyrant's one aim seems to have been to re-establish heathenism in Armenia, and to put down the religion of Christ in that country. In this, however, he entirely failed. Of the details of the contest we know but little, but it ended disastrously for Maximin and his army; and the triumph which they had thus gained over the dreaded legions must have tended still further to confirm the faith and increase the zeal of Tiridatês and his fellow-countrymen.

Sometime after the repulse of Maximin, Gregory and Tiridatês were cheered by a message from the monarch of Georgia, announcing his conversion to the Christian faith, and asking for teachers to carry on the work among his people. Georgia was at this time in a state of semi-dependence upon Armenia, and the news of the great events that had occurred in the latter country could not fail to produce an effect upon the minds of the inhabitants of the former. But the immediate occasion of the conversion of the people of Georgia is recorded by Moses of *Khoṛenê* and other Armenian writers in the following manner.

When Rhipsimê and her companions fled from Rome, some of the latter were scattered in various parts of the East. One of these was a nun called Nounê or Nouni, who went to Mds*kh*êth, the capital of Georgia, hoping to have an opportunity of preaching the Gospel there. Greek ecclesiastical writers say that she was captured and carried captive to that city, which seems the most reasonable of the two accounts. However this may have been, after many years' residence there her opportunity came at last. The Queen of Georgia's little son fell ill. Many wise women skilled in medicine were consulted by his anxious mother, but all to no purpose. The queen was almost in despair, when she at last heard of Nounê's skill in healing disease. Nounê was summoned to the palace, and asked to prescribe for the little sufferer. She saw at once that the only chance of saving the child's life lay in prayer. Kneeling down, therefore, by his couch, she prayed that Christ, who during His life on earth had healed so many, would graciously restore this little prince also to health and strength. Her petition was heard, and the child was immediately healed (a.d. 317). Shortly after this the queen herself was stricken with a severe malady. On Nounê's prayer, health was granted to her also. The King of Georgia, Miḥran by name, was warm in his expressions of gratitude, and offered to reward Nounê richly. She refused to receive any reward, giving all the glory to Christ her Master. This surprised the king, and enabled Nounê to proclaim her message to him also, as she had already done to his family. Though he listened with great attention and interest to her proclamation of the Gospel, and was also much struck by the narrative which he had heard regarding the martyrdom of her companions in Armenia, and the terrible punishment which had so soon afterwards befallen King Tiridatês, yet for a time no visible result followed. Miḥran still continued to serve the gods of his fathers.

One day, however, when he was out hunting, a thick fog arose, which caused Miḥran to be separated from his companions and attendants. The darkness increased, and the king completely lost his way. He called upon his gods to help him, but received no help from them. Under these circumstances—so the story runs—the king's mind reverted to what had occurred to Tiridatês. Conscious of many evil deeds which he had committed, he began to fear that he might be punished as the Armenian monarch had been. His guilty conscience, coupled with the failure of his gods to answer his prayer, induced Miḥṛan at last to turn to the true God, of whom Nounê had told him. Knowing by previous experience in his own household that God hears and answers prayer, Miḥṛan in his distress vowed that if God now interposed to scatter the darkness and enable him to escape from his dangerous position, he would give up the worship of idols and adore Him alone. His prayer was heard. The fog cleared away, and Miḥṛan reached home in safety.

True to his vow, the king now applied to Nounê for definite Christian teaching. She did all she could, and many of the people of the city turned to Christ. By her advice Miḥṛan now sent Gregory word of his conversion, and begged him to send preachers of the Gospel to instruct him and his people and to administer baptism to the converts. Overjoyed at the news, Gregory forthwith dispatched Christian evangelists to Georgia, giving orders that all the idols in the country should be destroyed, and that crosses should be erected in their stead. On a hill to the east of the city of Mds*kh*êth stood a gigantic image of the god Aṛamazd, whom the people adored every morning at sunrise. By Miḥṛan's command this was destroyed, and in its stead a roughly hewn wooden cross was erected. The story goes that the people mocked at the new symbol, and said that their forests were full of timber such as that. Thereupon Nounê prayed to the All-Merciful God to show them a sign of the superiority of the new faith and of the symbol which represented it. Instantly a pillar of cloud, bright and shining, descended from the sky and covered the hill on which the cross stood. Sweet odours breathed forth from the cloud, and angelic voices were heard giving glory to God. Gradually the cloud parted, and over the despised wooden cross there stood another, bright as the light, and crowned with twelve stars. All who beheld the wondrous sight ' were strengthened in their faith in Christ, and worshipped the holy cross.'

A later narrative relates that, by Nounê's advice, the king began to erect a Christian church in Mds*kh*êth. In the space of a year the building began to approach completion. When the columns were being raised by machinery, one of the chief of them refused to stir. Every effort to move it from the ground was in vain, and the machines used for the purpose were broken in the attempt. Hearing of this, Nounê visited the place alone by night, and prayed that some miraculous sign might be vouchsafed, to confirm the new converts in their faith. Thereupon the column rose of itself, or was raised by invisible hands, and stood on its pedestal, but without touching the latter. The king came early next morning to consult with the architect and the builders with regard to the best way of raising the column to its place. To their astonishment they beheld the pillar raised aloft in the air over the place assigned to it; and while they still gazed at the strange sight it quietly settled down on the pedestal prepared for it. Moved by this prodigy, all present cried aloud, ' True is that God whom Nounê preaches.'

The new faith quickly spread throughout Georgia, Nounê herself, whom Moses of Khoṛenê calls a female apostle, going from one end of the country to the other to proclaim the Gospel, and being nobly seconded in her efforts by the preachers and teachers who, in response to a new appeal made by Miḥṛan to both Constantine the Great and Tiridatês, were now coming in larger numbers to Georgia. Thus yet another Eastern nation received the Word of God, and turned from their idols to serve the Living God and to wait for His Son from heaven. Well might the zealous preachers of the Cross echo the words of the beloved disciple (1 John ii. 8), 'The darkness is passing away, and the true light already shineth.'

CHAPTER IX

CONCLUSION OF THE LIFE-WORK OF GREGORY AND TIRIDATÊS

' He who seeketh a thing and striveth findeth it, and he who knocketh at a door and persevereth entereth.'—*Arabic Proverb.*

We have seen that Gregory the Illuminator's retreat from the court of Tiridatês had caused great disquiet to the king himself and to the people at large. Gregory's influence had been so widespread and so effectual that men did not know how to do without him. On this account, Tiridatês made repeated applications to him to return and accompany him in his frequent journeys through the country, so that both king and people might have the benefit of his wisdom and experience in matters both religious and secular. But Gregory refused to accede to these entreaties, and expressed his intention of ending his days as a recluse.

While Tiridatês was almost in despair on this account, feeling that he himself alone as a secular ruler was quite unable to cope with the inevitable reaction in favour of heathen manners and lax morality which was even now becoming apparent among his subjects, and especially among the powerful nobles, a plan was suggested to him which seemed to promise good results. Up to this time the king was quite unaware that Gregory had ever married. But now some of the Illuminator's nearest friends informed Tiridatês that not only had Gregory been married in his early manhood, but also that his two sons, the fruit of that union, were living in Cappadocia. The plan which was suggested, and which commended itself to the king and also to the people at large, was to summon these sons of Gregory to Armenia, and to persuade Gregory to consecrate one or both of them to the office of archbishop in his own stead. Without informing Gregory himself of his intention, Tiridatês dispatched three nobles of the highest position to Caesarea with orders to prevail upon both of Gregory's sons[1] to come to the Armenian court. When these royal messengers arrived at Caesarea, they found Vṛthanês, the eldest, resident there, but the younger and more eminent of the two, Aṛistakês or Rĕstakês, was living as a hermit in the wilderness. Vṛthanês had at first adopted a secular life, but had now entered the ministry of the Church and been ordained presbyter. Aṛistakês, on the other hand, had from his earliest years been set apart for the 'religious ' life and had been dedicated to God's service. He had lived a life of self-denial and hardship, dwelling apart from men, inured to hunger and thirst, practising austerities, and gaining very great influence and esteem by his zeal and devotion.

Vṛthanês at once acceded to Tiridatês' request to go to Armenia and labour there ; but for some time Aṛistakês positively refused to leave his hermitage and mingle with the world. At last, however, he yielded to the advice of a large number of leading Christians of Cappadocia, who very wisely said to him, ' It is good for thee to toil in God's husbandry ; better far than living alone in the desert.' Tiridatês' envoys returned in triumph to their master, bringing the two young men with them. The king received them with much honour, and at once started with them to find their father, who was then residing in a desert place in a cave among the Manayaṛkh Mountains in the canton of Daṛanaghikh. When they were admitted to Gregory's presence, the king very strongly urged upon the hermit that, as he had repeatedly and steadfastly refused to leave his retirement and once more to go in and out among the people, he should at least consecrate his son Rĕstakês as archbishop in his stead. This was done (a.d. 317), and after his father's death Rĕstakês assumed the title of ' Katholicos,' which is still borne by the head of the Armenian Church. It is generally said that he was the first who bore the title, but Agathangelos sometimes uses it in reference to Gregory himself. During the rest of Gregory's lifetime, however, Rĕstakês acted as his coadjutor; for Gregory continued his labours up to the very end, constantly moving about the country in his hermit garb, preaching and teaching the people. Tiridatês himself aided in the work, living a holy and self-sacrificing life, and endeavouring by his devotion to Christ's service to obliterate from the minds of others—as he never could from his own—the remembrance of his earlier sins and his opposition to the spread of the Gospel.

The glad news of the conversion of Constantine the Great to the Christian faith had now reached Armenia. Nothing could exceed Tiridatês' joy and thankfulness to God when he learnt that the true faith had now triumphed in the Roman empire also, and that there now sat on the imperial throne an emperor who bowed the knee to Christ. What a change from the time when, not many years before, Tiridatês himself, placed on the throne by an imperial persecutor, had thought it his duty to obey no less the mandate of the emperor than the impulse of his own heathen zeal by instituting a relentless persecution of those who professed the faith of Christ crucified ! Now the thrones of Byzantium, Armenia and Georgia alike were occupied by Christian sovereigns. Constantine had completely vanquished his foes, and inflicted upon Western heathenism what, it might well be hoped, would prove to be its death-blow. Christianity, though amid fearful persecutions, was making great progress in Persia, and news was soon to come that far Ethiopia too had stretched out her hands unto God. In Arabia, India, and among the Goths of Moesia too, the faith was rapidly spreading. The darkness, it seemed, must everywhere soon give place to the dawn of truth and righteousness.

Tiridatês resolved on going in person to Rome to tender his homage to Constantine and to congratulate him upon his accession. Accordingly in A.D. 318 he marched out of Vagharshapat with an army of 70,000 men, accompanied by Gregory, Rĕstakês, and Bishop Albinus, and also the chief nobles in the kingdom, with the intention of going to Rome by way of Cappadocia. When the king reached the canton of Taṛôn, messengers from the ruler of Georgia reached his camp, begging for help to enable him to repel a formidable invasion of the Huns and other Sarmatian tribes, who had entered Georgia and were laying the country waste with fire and sword. Tiridatês at once dispatched an army of 30,000 men to the assistance of his ally. The invaders were beaten back with great loss, and many leading chiefs were taken captive. Tiridatês was therefore free to continue his journey, with a reasonable hope that Armenia would have nothing to fear from any foreign invader until his return. He was received with much honour by Constantine, and returned to Armenia with valuable gifts, which he handed over to the Church.

Sapor I, King of Persia, had meanwhile taken advantage of Tiridatês' absence from the country to make an attack on Armenia. He induced a powerful chief named Sghouk to rise in rebellion, and easily succeeded in persuading the Scythian tribes, headed by Gedṛeḥon, King of the Huns, to invade the country. Dṛov, the Armenian general who commanded the army stationed on the northern border for the defence of Georgia, was bribed to retire from his position and leave the way open for Gedṛeḥon and his savage hordes.

On doing this, Dṛov went and joined Sghouk, who had meanwhile slain the loyal general Ôta (his own son-in-law), and captured the fortress of Oghkan, in the canton of Taṛôn. The mountaineers of Mount Sim joined the rebels, and the whole country was thrown into confusion, and seemed little likely to succeed in repelling the army with which Sapor was preparing to march upon the capital. At this crisis King Tiridatês fortunately returned to Armenia (A.D. 319). In the plain of Gaṛgaṛa, Tiridatês, with only 30,000 troops, met in battle an immense host of northern invaders.

For a time the victory hung in the balance, but Gregory's prayers and the relics of the apostles which he had brought from Rome cheered the Armenian army, and enabled them to gain a decisive victory. Tiridatês displayed prowess worthy of his old reputation, cutting Gedṛeḥon in two with one mighty sword-stroke, and pursuing the flying remnants of his army to the frontiers of Sarmatia. During the next two years, however, the country was troubled by fresh inroads of these barbarians.

Tiridatês then turned against his rebellious subjects. Sghouk was murdered by a treacherous friend whom he unwisely trusted, exactly as King *Khoṣrov* had been assassinated by Anak many years previously. Tiridatês rewarded the murderer, Mangoun, by bestowing on him the canton of Taṛôn and ennobling his family, a deed most unworthy of a Christian king.

It was now necessary for the king to repel the Persian invaders. But he had lost so many men that Tiridatês thought it needful to await the arrival of the Roman auxiliaries whom he had been promised.

Meanwhile he reorganized his army. The generalissimo of Armenia, Aṛtavazd Mandakouni, had recently fallen in battle. Tiridatês therefore abolished that office and returned to the old Armenian system of dividing the army into four separate forces, each under its own head, independent of every other general. The four generals now appointed were Miḥṛan, King or Prince of Georgia and Gongaria ; Vaḥan Amatouni ; Manachiḥṛ Rshtouni ; and Bagaṛat Bagṛatouni. The disadvantage of this arrangement was that it formed four distinct armies, unlikely to co-operate well with one another, as they had no common head. In after times this caused great injury to the country.

When the Roman army was ready to take the field, it marched into Syria, to assail Sapor from that quarter. At the same time Tiridatês attacked the north-western part of the Persian empire, and conquered a large part of Atropatenê, including the city of Tabriz, which he strongly fortified. He also recovered some other minor portions of Armenian territory which the Persians had occupied. Assaulted from two different quarters, Sapor was compelled to sue for peace. This was granted ; and Tiridatês, leaving a garrison in Tabriz, returned home.

Soon after Constantine had proclaimed Christianity to be the established religion of the Roman empire (A.D. 324), he sent out circular letters inviting all the bishops throughout his dominions to attend the meeting of the First General Council of the Church, which was held at Nicaea in Bithynia in A.D. 325. An invitation was sent to Gregory also, but he felt that he could not leave Armenia, and therefore he, with the consent of Tiridatês, sent his son and coadjutor Aṛistakês to the council instead. As is well known, Arianism was condemned at Nicaea, and the earlier form of the Nicene Creed (i.e. the Nicene Creed properly so called, as distinct from the clauses added later) was adopted by the council. Aṛistakês, on his return to Armenia, brought with him a copy of the canons of the council, including the newly formulated creed. Gregory thereupon assembled a synod of the Armenian bishops at Vagharṣhapat (a.d. 325), which adopted the Nicene Creed and the twenty canons for the better government of the Church drawn up at Nicaea, adding others which seemed especially desirable for Armenia.

Gregory had now seen the Church thoroughly established and Christianity adopted as the national religion of Armenia. The meeting of the council at Vagharṣhapat, and their adoption of the same creed as that drawn up and accepted by the Nicene Council, seemed to him to remove any real danger of the growth of the Arian heresy in the country. The Church in Armenia was independent and thoroughly national : it now had a constitution and canons, and gave promise of great progress. Gregory therefore felt that his work was done. He was now an aged man in failing health, and his son Aṛistakês seemed well able to carry on alone the labours in which he had for years past so zealously assisted his father. Gregory had therefore no scruple in resigning the patriarchate into his son's hands, and retiring into the life of seclusion which he so much loved. This he now did. He selected as his hermitage the cave of Mankh in Mount Sepouḥ, and withdrawing to it, finally disappeared from the sight of men. He died there peacefully in A.D. 332. Some shepherds found and buried his body in that neighbourhood. It was afterwards removed to the village of Thoṛdan, and later still to Vagharṣhapat. His name has ever since been honoured by the Armenian Church as that of one of the very best and most glorious of the saints of God, and several festivals are held every year in commemoration of Gregory 'the Illuminator,' the Apostle of the Armenian nation.

Almost immediately after Gregory's decease, the ancient paganism—at least as far as regarded morality —began to endeavour to reassert itself in Armenia. Many of the people were Christians only in name, while in heart they still clung to the licence which heathenism permitted to its devotees. Such men had been to a great degree restrained during Gregory's lifetime from venturing openly to violate the principles of Christian morality. The influence which Gregory exercised over the whole nation had been too great to permit any one openly to defy his authority, especially as he was supported by the king. But Gregory was now dead, and King Tiridatês was aged and feeble, and no longer able to punish any transgression of the moral law on the part of the more powerful of the nobles. Aṛistakês, who on his father's death had assumed the full authority of Katholicos, was a good and pious man, but he had not his father's influence. All his efforts and those of the king to arrest the recrudescence of pagan practices to a large extent failed. The nobles refused to listen to the remonstrances of the Katholicos, and some of them openly began to indulge in polygamy and other customs which they had been unwillingly compelled to give up when they were baptized. The example was not lost upon the common people, and all who had for years yielded a reluctant obedience to the precepts of the Church now threw off the mask and showed themselves in their true colours. It was a revulsion of feeling in religious matters somewhat similar to that which occurred in England on the accession of Charles II, when Puritan austerity and rigid decorum gave way to an outbreak of the most shameless licentiousness and irreligion. Aṛistakês did not shrink from his duty, though conscious of the danger which he was incurring. He boldly reproved offenders, however exalted their position and however great their power and influence might be. The struggle did not last long, and the victory (as in all such cases) seemed for the moment to rest with the evildoers, whereas the apparent success of wickedness in reality paved the way for its overthrow. One of the leading nobles, Archelaus by name, the ruler of Armenia Quarta, had committed some flagrant breach of the moral law ; and Aṛistakês, like another John the Baptist, felt it his duty to reprove him openly, and to endeavour to lead him to repentance. Leaving the capital therefore, the Katholicos, attended by a small retinue, set out to visit that province. On the way he was met in the district of Dsophkh by emissaries of Archelaus, who cruelly murdered him (a.d. 340). His body was removed to the town of Thil, in the canton of Ekeghikh, which place Tiridatês had given to Gregory, and where Aṛistakês had erected a monastery for his own residence. A plot was shortly afterwards made to murder Aṛistakês' elder brother Vṛthanês also in the canton of Taṛôn ; but his life was providentially preserved, as we shall see a little later.

The murder of Aṛistakês and the troubles which were now threatening to engulf the Church of Armenia, coupled with his own age and his inability to cope with these disorders, all combined to render Tiridatês weary of the world. His one desire now was to depart in peace to the more immediate presence of the Saviour, whose disciples he had at one time so cruelly persecuted, but whom he had long since learned to love, and whose Gospel he had vied with Gregory himself in spreading throughout the whole kingdom. The king therefore, while awaiting his home-call, resolved to retire from the world, as Gregory, his friend and counsellor, had done. He betook himself therefore (apparently very soon after Aṛistakês ' murder) to the cave of Mankh, which had formed Gregory's last earthly residence, and there resolved to pass the few remaining days of his life as a hermit, far removed from the cares and trials of the world.

The state of confusion and lawlessness, which had been steadily growing worse in Armenia during the time that had elapsed since Gregory's death, was naturally heightened by the king's abdication. The Persian king was waiting for a favourable opportunity of attacking the country, and Tiridatês' sons were not possessed of sufficient force of character to give the people much confidence in their ability to rule firmly and well, even should one of them be appointed by the court of Constantinople to fill his father's place. Fearing the outbreak of a civil war and the attacks of their external foes, the nobles met in council, and resolved to visit Tiridatês in his hermitage and induce him to resume the reins of government. They accordingly went to the cave in Mount Sepouḥ where the king dwelt, and endeavoured by every means in their power to prevail upon him to accede to their request. But Tiridatês steadily refused, and persisted in devoting the rest of his days to religious retirement. Angered at their failure, some of the nobles secretly caused him to be poisoned, in the eighty-fifth year of his life and the fifty-sixth of his reign (a. d. 342), and thereby, as an Armenian historian writes, they ' quenched for them-selves the brightly shining ray of the service of God.' Tiridatês was one of the greatest and noblest Kings of Armenia. His great strength of body, his bravery and martial prowess, his firmness and decision of character, his moral courage in specially difficult and trying circumstances, his fidelity to his friends and to the cause of duty, and lastly his deep piety and fervent zeal for the spread of the Gospel of Christ—all this, coupled with wisdom and experience of no common order, and with hearty and devoted patriotism, combined to render him one of the ablest monarchs that ever sat on the throne of the Armenian Arsacides.

The king's funeral was in the style usual with the monarchs of his line. The body of the deceased sovereign was reverently laid upon a kind of bier or litter covered with silver, and to this four snow-white mules with golden trappings were yoked. His family, relatives and friends, together with two ranks of soldiers in full armour, surrounded the bier. In the front of the funeral *cortège* there marched a Christian choir, singing the hymns of hope and joy which Tiridatês had so much loved during his lifetime. Censers breathed forth incense in clouds, and the music of the harp and of the trumpet accompanied the monarch to his long home. Behind followed the usual throng of hired female mourners, wailing and beating their breasts. An immense multitude of the common people brought up the rear. The body was finally laid to rest—at least for a time—in a marble sarcophagus in the village of Thoṛdan, the last resting-place of Gregory, his lifelong friend and guide.

CHAPTER X

CHARACTERISTICS OF THE CHRISTIANITY INTRO-DUCED INTO ARMENIA BY GREGORY AND HIS COMPANIONS

'Sapientiam sibi adimunt, qui sine ullo iudicio inventa maiorum probant, et ab aliis pecudum more ducuntur. . . . Quid ergo impedit, quin ab ipsis sumamus exemplum; ut, quomodo illi, quae falsa invenerant, posteris tradiderunt, sic nos, qui verum invenimus, posteris meliora tradamus ? '—Lactantius, *Divin. Inst.* ii. 8.

In the last few chapters we have seen under what circumstances the Christian faith ultimately succeeded in becoming the national religion of the Armenian people at a date earlier than that of the conversion of any other nation, whether Eastern or Western. In the course of our narrative we have been enabled casually to notice some of the distinguishing characteristics of the form of Christianity preached by Gregory and his followers. But it will be well to study this subject more in detail, since the religion of Armenia to the present day professes to be the same as that preached by the ' Illuminator,' and is doubtless very largely based upon it.

Gregory and his assistants were connected both with the Church of Syria and with that of the Roman world, but perhaps more especially with the former. Syrian influence certainly prevailed very largely in Armenia for several centuries after his time, and the Syrian language was much more familiar to the clergy and people than was the Greek. It is well known that (as was the case with the Persian Church during the same period) the Scriptures were for many years read in the Syriac language in public worship, and explained in the vernacular. This fact has left its marks upon the language and religion of the country up to the present time. Bishop Lightfoot has well pointed out that, although our knowledge of the early history of the Syrian Church is comparatively scanty, yet the most ancient documents which refer to it 'exhibit a high sacerdotal view of the episcopate as prevailing' in it 'from the earliest times of which any record is preserved[1].' Quite in accordance with this, we find Agathangelos, Faustus Byzantinus and other early Armenian chroniclers speaking of Gregory and his successors in the office of Katholicos as the ' High priests of God,' the ' Chief priests of the Armenian nation.' The word most commonly used in ancient Armenian and almost exclusively employed in the modern language to denote a Christian presbyter is *khaḥanah,* obviously the Syriac *kâhnâ* or *kohno,* the Hebrew a sacrificial priest *(sacerdos, sacrificulus).* Of course this word is not used in the Peshiṭṭâ version to denote a Christian minister or elder *(πρεσβύτερος),* being carefully restricted in its application to Jewish and heathen priests. But in comparatively early times the Syrian Church fell into the error of confounding the Christian ministry with the Jewish priesthood, and thus this very serious corruption of the truth was introduced into the Armenian Church from its very foundation as the Church of the nation. This is the more deeply to be regretted because the Christian Church, properly speaking, ' has no sacerdotal system .' It would be hard to find any heresy that has ever spread so widely throughout Christendom, and which yet is so utterly without the shadow of a foundation in the writings of the New Testament. We, however, who in our own sad experience have witnessed the rise and growth of this error among professed members of the Church of England in our own day and genera-tion, can hardly wonder that it gained ground so rapidly in the early Church. ' Though no distinct traces of sacerdotalism are visible in the ages imme-diately after the apostles, yet, having once taken root in the Church, it shot up rapidly into maturity. Towards the close of the second century we discern the first germs appearing above the surface ; yet shortly after the middle of the third the plant has all but attained its full growth .'

The belief in the sacerdotal character of the Christian ministry in fact seems to have been ' imported into Christianity by the ever-increasing mass of heathen converts, who were incapable of shaking off their sacerdotal prejudices and apprehending the free spirit of the Gospel .' . . . ' For the heathen, familiar with auguries, lustrations, sacrifices, and depending on the intervention of some priest for all the manifold religious rights of the state, the clan, and the family, the sacerdotal func-tions must have occupied a far larger space in the affairs of everyday life, than for the Jew of the Dispersion, who of necessity dispensed, and had no scruple at dispensing, with priestly ministrations from one year's end to the other. With this presumption, drawn from probability, the evidence of fact accords. In Latin Christendom, as represented by the Church of Carthage, the germs of the sacerdotal idea appear first, and soonest ripen to maturity. If we could satisfy ourselves of the early date of the ancient Syriac documents lately published, we should have discovered another centre from which this idea was propagated. And so far their testimony may perhaps be accepted. Syria was at least a soil where such a plant would thrive and luxuriate. In no country of the civilized world was sacerdotal authority among the heathen greater. The most important centres of Syrian Christianity, Antioch and Emesa, were also the cradles of strongly-marked sacerdotal religions which at different times made their influence felt throughout the Roman empire. This being so, it is a significant fact that the first instance of the term "priest " *(iepevs),* applied to a Christian minister, occurs in a heathen writer . . . . But though the *spirit* which imported the idea into the Church of Christ and sustained it there was chiefly due to Gentile education, yet its *form* was almost as certainly derived from the Old Testament. And this is the modification which needs to be made in the statement, in itself substantially true, that sacerdotalism must be traced to the influence of heathen rather than of Jewish converts.

Some of the measures adopted by Gregory for the establishment and speedy propagation of the Christian faith in Armenia, though doubtless undertaken with the best motives, tended still further to lead the infant Armenian Church to accept and retain the sacerdotal error which Gregory himself, in common with so many Christians of his day, accepted as undoubted truth. For example, Agathangelos informs us that Gregory, when the heathen priests were converted and seemed suitable for the work, often ordained *the same men* to ' the Christian priesthood ' that had very shortly before held that of the heathen gods, and he not unfrequently appointed them to conduct divine service and ' offer the sacrifice ' (i. e. administer the sacrament of the Lord's Supper) in the very place where they had not long previously acted as the sacrificial priests of the pagan deities. It was, as we have already seen, Gregory's policy and constant practice to erect Christian churches and monasteries and shrines in honour of the saints and martyrs on the sites of the heathen temples which he had razed to the ground. Acting doubtless at his request, or at least with his approval, King Tiridatês dedicated to the support of these shrines and other ecclesiastical foundations the landed property and other possessions of the pagan temples which they had replaced. The heathen festivals held at these places were not abolished, but, in lieu of men assembling there to worship Vaḥagn or Mihr, they now came together in honour of John the Baptist or some other Christian saint. Where pilgrimages to sacred sites used to be made, they were still continued, but a reason was invented for them in accordance with some monkish legend. The images of the heathen deities were shattered, but in their stead the cross and the relics of the martyrs were substituted as fitting objects of adoration. Of course the subtle distinction between *δουλεία* and *λατρεία* was inculcated and insisted on, as is still the case in the Armenian as well as in the Greek and Roman Churches. But equally of course, the minds of most men, especially such as had only very recently been converted from polytheism, failed to observe the distinction very accurately. It is hardly too much to say, therefore, that one system of polytheism was exchanged for another in the estimation of the great mass of the people. The churches were filled with dense crowds of baptized heathen, mingled among whom were a few really earnest and enlightened Christians. The names of the objects of worship were entirely changed, and the forms and ceremonies were in most cases of necessity abolished and others substituted. But the people in general were, perhaps, conscious of little more alteration than this.

The great advantage which the proselytes gained was the opportunity of hearing the Gospel fully and freely preached. Much of sacerdotalism may be found in Gregory's teaching (if we regard as in any degree genuine the sermons bearing his name which have come down to us). But, nevertheless, he and many of the clergy he brought with him from Syria and Asia Minor most earnestly and simply proclaimed, with great and fervent zeal and love, the good news of salvation through Christ Jesus' atoning death. The revelation of the Fatherhood and love of God as mani-fested in His Son, and the promulgation of the moral law as in harmony with the nature of God Most High and Holy, were advantages of quite inestimable value, and still render the most corrupt form of Christianity infinitely superior to the very loftiest and purest of non-Christian religions. Nor was such preaching in vain. Many of those who had at first confessed Christ from more or less mixed motives were doubtless truly converted after a time. Gregory never baptized without giving his converts as full and careful instruction as opportunity permitted. One result of this was a moral reformation in Armenia. Vice was sternly condemned, and the general moral tone of the community was distinctly raised. Those who, like Tiridatês, accepted the Gospel with all their hearts endeavoured to walk henceforth in newness of life. In spite of the fact that Tiridatês almost forcibly suppressed heathenism and brought pressure to bear upon some of his subjects in order to induce them to embrace Christianity, yet the very fact that he was able to succeed in his attempt to do so, though at the time the whole power of the heathen priesthood within the country, and the determined opposition to and hatred of Christianity on the part of the rulers of both the Roman and Persian empires without, were arrayed against him in that matter, shows that the heart of the nation was with him in his desire to cast off the fetters of paganism and to adopt as the national faith the religion of Christ. This was still more clearly-proved by the permanence of Christianity in the country. The recrudescence of heathenism after Gregory's death did much harm, and cost the lives of several eminent martyrs, among whom more than one of his successors in the archiepiscopal dignity were numbered. Yet it entirely failed to overthrow Christianity in Armenia and to restore the worship of the heathen deities. Nor have all the persecutions that Christians have since suffered in that land, from the time of the ' Holy Vaṛdans ' up to the terrible massacres which the last few years have witnessed, sufficed to extinguish the light of Christian truth. This shows that, however serious may have been the doctrinal errors of the Church (which were in some measure present even in Gregory's own days), there has always been much that is real and earnest in the Christianity of the Armenian people.

We must not pass over a very important result of the preaching of the Gospel in Armenia, and one which was clearly in Gregory's mind from the very beginning of his work in that land. We have seen that there was but little indigenous vernacular literature in existence in the country before its conversion to the Christian faith. It was not until some considerable time after Gregory's death that the present Armenian alphabet was invented by his disciples, and the Bible translated into the language of the people. Yet the schools for the study of Greek and Syriac, which Gregory opened in various parts of the country, were the places where, in some measure, the men were trained who ultimately gave the people that ' Queen of Versions,' the ancient Armenian Bible, which is still read in the churches of the land. In the case of Armenia, as in that of many another land, the Bible itself practically formed the beginning of its literature, as we shall see when we come to consider the history of Mesṛop and his coadjutors.

It will be plain from what we have already said that Armenia has never, until quite recent times, had an opportunity of accepting genuine and uncorrupted Christianity. Sacerdotal heresy and the worship of images, pictures, the cross, the relics of the martyrs and the saints, have ever since Gregory's time been at work in that Church to lead men away from the simplicity of the Gospel of Christ. Viewing the history of Israel as recorded for us by inspired men in the Old Testament, *one* cannot help being led to believe that the terrible misery and oppression which for more than a millennium has been the lot of the Armenian nation at large, and which has scattered them, like the Hebrews, throughout almost the whole world, has been in God's inscrutable Providence permitted for much the same reason as that which accounts for almost the same fate having befallen the Jews. Idolatry always caused the chosen people of God to be punished and scattered far and wide among the heathen in days of yore. Saint and image worship, and the practice of substituting a weak and imperfect man in the place of Christ Himself as our mediator, have brought degradation and misery upon every Christian nation that has fallen into such errors. The history of Spain, of Italy, of Greece and of Armenia are only fresh illustrations of the working of the Divine Law, which is written in such large characters upon the biblical narrative of the history of Israel. But as no nation of the world has, alike in its zeal for its religion and in its misfortunes, so closely resembled Israel as the ill-fated ' house of Togarmah' has done, may we not believe that, for them as for Israel, there is still in store a glorious future, which will cause past misery and oppression to be remembered no more, and in which, purified by the fire of affliction, both these nations, the first Semitic and the first Âryan nation to turn to God, will work together to spread far and wide throughout the world the knowledge of the unsearchable riches of Christ ?

CHAPTER XI

SUCCESSORS OF GREGORY AND OF TIRIDATES

Καθάπερ πλοῖον ἐν θαλάττῃ την ἐκκλησίαν ἐν τῇ οἰκουμένῃ φέρεσθαι πάλιν ἀφεῖτ, οὐ κατέλυσε την ζάλην [ὁ Χριστός], ἀλλ' ἐξήρπασε της ζάλης οὐ κατέστειλε την θάλασσαν, ἀλλ' ἠσφαλίσατο την ναυν.—Chrysostom, *Hom, in Princ. Act.* ii. 1.

On the death of Tiridatês a period of internal discord and confusion followed in Armenia. Tiridatês himself had, towards the end of his life, found the turbulent nobles beyond his power to restrain and render obedient to his commands ; and the fact of his retiring from public life without making any arrangement for the government of the country did not tend to reduce matters to order. On the murder of Tiridatês, his eldest son, *Khosṛov* II, became rightful King of Armenia. But he for some years entirely failed to make his authority and power felt. There was no settled government in the land, and each of the greater nobles did what was right in his own eyes. The defenceless state of the country encouraged the northern tribes to renew their plundering incursions, as they were ready to do whenever opportunity occurred. As a natural result Armenia was filled with bloodshed and confusion, in which both Church and State seemed destined to be wrecked.

One of the first and most dangerous enemies with whom *Khosṛov* II had to contend was Sanaṭrouk or Sanêsan , King of the Mazkhouthians, a tribe living on the western shore of the Caspian Sea, beyond the ' Caspian Gates,' to the south of the river Gerros. This chief was a noble of the royal family of the Arsacides, and as such was a relative of *Khosṛov* himself. Sanaṭrouk had been sent to that region by Tiridatês, and appointed governor of that part of the Armenian territories. The population of those regions was formed of a large number of different tribes, the Huns, the Alvanians, &c, speaking different languages, and always ready at a favourable opportunity to shake off the Armenian yoke. Moses of Khoṛenê informs us that the people of the province of Phaitakaṛan, on the coast of the Caspian, but south of the Caucasus, had entreated King Tiridatês to give them as their bishop some one of the descendants of Gregory the Illuminator; and that the king, when sending Sanaṭrouk to his northern province, had at the same time sent to Phaitakaṛan Gṛegoṛis, son of Vṛthanês and grandson of the Illuminator. Gṛegoṛis was at the time of his consecration only fifteen years of age, but his wisdom and ability were far beyond his years, and gave promise of a life worthy of his noble origin. His diocese had no very clearly-marked boundaries, but included Georgia, Alvania, Phaitakaṛan and the district north of the Caucasus. He is described by Faustus Byzantinus as a man full of zeal and earnestness, somewhat stern and austere, of pure and noble life, a most devoted preacher of the Gospel, perfectly indefatigable in his work, accustomed to self-denial and to toiling night and day in God's service, and resolved to preach to men far and near the divine message entrusted to him. He restored decayed churches and built new ones wher-ever he went, and endeavoured to put down all lingering attachment to idolatry. He visited Âzarbâijân, where most of the people were still attached to the Magian faith, and having preached the Gospel to them, turned his steps to the court of Sanaṭrouk, longing to bring to those wild and barbarous tribes the good news of salvation. His zeal and missionary spirit, however, were the immediate cause of a singularly fierce onslaught on Armenia, which came about in the following manner.

The wonderful news which Gṛegoṛis preached with such zeal and earnestness at first carried conviction to the minds of the inhabitants of those wild regions. They felt that the message must be true ; and the fact that within the last few years Christianity had become the established religion of the Roman empire and of Armenia, while the sound of the Gospel was heard even among some of their neighbours to the north of the Black Sea, led them to perceive that the religion which Gṛegoṛis preached must in the end prevail. For a time, therefore, they acknowledged its truth, and it seemed as if they would follow the example of the Georgians and ask for baptism *en masse.* But when they learnt more of the fruits of the Gospel, and heard from Gṛegoṛis that, if they became Christians, they must abstain from murder and adultery, from coveting their neighbours' goods, from making raids into the neighbouring territories and pillaging them, carrying away as slaves all of their inhabitants whom they had not slaughtered, the fierce and warlike spirit of these barbarians asserted itself. 'Why,' they cried, 'if we accept this new faith, we shall not have courage even to mount our horses ! How can we who are so numerous manage to exist if we do not plunder our richer neighbours? ' The discontent spread, and the people at last became convinced that Gṛegoṛis had been sent to them by the Armenian monarch with the hope of deceiving them, and preventing them from ever renewing their predatory

incursions into his territories. They therefore resolved to murder Gṛegoṛis, and to make such an attack upon Armenia as had not been made within living memory.
Sanatṛouk's ambition led him to fall in with this plan. He had heard of the troubled state of Armenia and the weakness of *Khosṛov* 'Kotak ' (' the small '), as the new king was entitled from his diminutive stature, and he hoped to make himself, if not King of Armenia, at least independent monarch of the northern tribes. He therefore assumed the crown and the title of king, and collected a countless host of Huns, Alvanians and other tribes, in order to invade *Khosṛov's* dominions. But Gṛegoṛis must first be put to death. The barbarians therefore seized him and bound him to the tail of a wild horse, which they then released and pursued on the level ground near the northern shore of the Caspian. In this manner Gṛegoṛis bravely met a martyr's death when he was still quite a young man. His companions reverently interred his body at the town of Amaṛaz or Amaṛên in Little Siunikh, in a church built there by his grandfather, Gregory the Illuminator. His memory was kept green by a yearly festival or pilgrimage made to his tomb by people from all the surrounding country (a. d. 348).
After the murder of Aṛistakês, Gregory's younger son and successor in the office of Katholicos of Armenia, Vṛthanês, the elder son, became patriarch. The new Katholicos was animated by the same spirit which Gregory had shown in his work, and which distinguished all his descendants except two, as we shall see in the course of our narrative. Vṛthanês at once commenced a systematic visitation of all the churches, and everywhere endeavoured to keep alight the fire of Christian faith and zeal in the breasts of the people. All the great ecclesiastics of early Armenian history are famed for their sermons, many of which are still preserved to us. In this respect they differ from the Armenian clergy of the present day, many of whom never preach at all.
Shortly after *Khosṛov*'s accession, an attempt was made on Vṛthanês' life. He had gone to visit the ' mother of all the churches of Armenia,' founded by Gregory the Illuminator on the spot where the idol temples had formerly stood in the canton of Taṛôn, near Mount Khaṛkhê, not far from the city of Ashtishat. Seven times a year a great festival used to be celebrated there in honour of John the Baptist, and many persons used then to make a pilgrimage to the spot, as their fathers had done in heathen times in honour of the pagan deities formerly worshipped there. Many still secretly clung to the old rites, and the descendants of the heathen priests who lived there were ready to make every effort to put down Christianity by every means in their power. The Queen of Armenia, wife of *Khosṛov* II, had been reproved by Vṛthanês, in the spirit of John the Baptist himself, for immorality, and she therefore in revenge incited the heathen in that neighbourhood to make an attack upon Vṛthanês while he was holding divine service in the church already spoken of. About 2,000 men surrounded the building and prepared for an assault on it. But, if we may credit Faustus Byzantinus and Moses of Khoṛenê, the hands of the assailants were suddenly bound behind their backs by invisible agency, and all their efforts to free themselves were unavailing. While they struggled in vain with their bonds, Vṛthanês came out of the church and asked them what they wanted and why they had come. Struck with remorse and guilty terror, the conspirators fell on their faces at his feet and confessed their evil design. Vṛthanês found them now convinced that his was the only true faith ; he therefore prayed for them, and they were set free. At their request he then instructed them in the faith of Christ ; and, after due preparation, they all, with their wives and children, soon after received baptism.
Shortly after this, two great nobles disturbed the peace of the country by their disputes. These were the Manavazean and the Oṛdouni clans. They took up arms against one another, pillaging and wasting each other's demesnes and causing great slaughter. *Khosṛov* sent Vṛthanês and Bishop Albinus to endeavour to make peace between them, but they insulted the king's messengers and drove them away. *Khosṛov* then sent Vachhê, son of his father's old guardian Aṛtavazd Mandakouni, the most distinguished general in the country at that time, to punish the rebels. This he did most effectually. He completely destroyed both of these noble families, putting every one of them to the sword, leaving ' neither male nor female cub ' alive. The estates of the Manavazeans near the river Euphrates were bestowed on Bishop Albinus, and those of the Oṛdounis on the bishops of the district of Basan, where they were situated.
The Katholicos Vṛthanês had still surviving one of his two sons, Housik, brother of the Gṛegoṛis whose martyrdom we have already recorded. Housik was brought up in the family of Tiṛan, *Khosṛov*'s son and heir. When he was still very young, Tiṛan gave Housik his daughter in marriage. Of this marriage twin sons were born, who bore the names Pap and Athanaginês. Before their birth Housik was informed by a vision that they would turn out vicious and worthless men. Grieved beyond measure by this information, Housik separated from his wife, who soon after died. While praying for his young sons, an angel appeared to him to comfort him with the promise that, though these sons of his would be worthless men, yet their children would return to the noble traditions of Gregory's family. 'Their progeny,' said the angel, 'shall be fountains of spiritual wisdom for Armenia, and from them shall well forth the graces enjoined by God's commandments. Much peace and prosperity and abundant confirmation of the Churches shall be given them from the Lord, with great success and power ; and many wanderers shall through them return into the way of truth, wherefore also through them Christ shall be glorified by many tongues. They shall be pillars of the Churches and stewards of the Word of life.' The angel went on to say that, amid the fiery furnace of affliction, they would stand firm as a rock, but after their days lying and deceit should flourish in the land. His message comforted Housik, who thanked God and took courage.
When news reached Armenia that Sanatṛouk had assumed the crown and made himself master of Phaitakaṛan, other rebellions broke out in various parts of the country. One of these was headed by one of the highest nobles in the country, Bakouṛ, chief of the Aghtznians, who invited the assistance of Sapor II, King of Persia. The latter advanced

towards the cantons of Ḥêṛ and Zaṛavand, whither *Khosṛov* dispatched a large force under Databen to oppose him. Databen basely plotted with the Persians, undertaking to betray *Khosṛov* into their hands, and actually enabled them to lead his own army into an ambush, in which 40,000 Armenians perished. The fugitives brought the sad news to *Khosṛov*, who was thus enabled to elude the traitor's schemes. Holding a council of the nobles, at which Vṛthanês was present, it was resolved to entreat the assistance of Constantius, who was himself at war with Sapor. With this object, a letter was sent to Constantius, entreating him to recognize *Khosṛov* as King of Armenia, to send the latter the customary crown and pallium which the Armenian sovereigns received from the Emperors of Rome, and to march to his assistance as soon as possible. Meanwhile *Khosṛov* sent an army of 30,000 men under Vachhê to repel the advancing Persians. The two armies met on the banks of a little river near the town of Arestn, not far from the shores of Lake Van. The huge host of the Persians was completely routed with terrible slaughter, and an immense quantity of booty, together with numerous captives and many elephants, was taken by the victors. The traitor Databên was captured alive and brought before the king, by whose orders he was stoned to death. According to the barbarous custom of the times, Vachhê was ordered to proceed to the island of Aghthamaṛ, where Databên's wife and family resided, and to put them all to the sword. This was done, and the property of the ill-fated family was confiscated.

Constantius agreed to the request of the Armenian nobles, and sent a general named Antiochus with a large army to their assistance, presenting *Khosṛov* also with the customary emblems of sovereignty. He was crowned by Antiochus in a.d. 344. *Khosṛov*, besides being small of stature, was weakly and unfit for war, so that he was unable to cope with the turbulent nobles of his time. But Antiochus had orders to thoroughly pacify the country ; and with a view to doing this and strengthening *Khosṛov* on the throne, he put the military affairs of Armenia into order, confirming in their positions the four generals of the four separate armies appointed by Tiridatês on the death of Aṛtavazd, and sending each of them with his army and an auxiliary Roman force to guard the special frontier assigned to them. Antiochus himself marched against Sanatṛouk, who reigned in the city of Phaitakaṛan, and obliged him to flee and take refuge with the Persian monarch. Meanwhile Manachiḥṛ, the general in command of the force entrusted with the protection of the southern provinces of Armenia, had defeated and slain Bakouṛ, and put to the sword his sons, brothers, and his whole house, with the exception of an infant daughter and one son. The latter fled to Vachhê, who protected him. The former was afterwards given in marriage to a noble named Vaghinek, who in right of his wife inherited the honours and estates of the family. Manachiḥṛ treated the whole of the cantons involved in the rebellion with terrible cruelty, not even exempting the serfs from slaughter. He carried away many captives, including eight deacons who were under the authority of the celebrated Jacob, Bishop of Nisibis. On the latter's protest, Manachiḥṛ incited the people of that part of the country to drown these unfortunate men. Hearing of this, Jacob went up to the top of a mountain, whence the whole region could be seen, and called down a curse upon Manachiḥṛ and the canton in which the murderers dwelt. This resulted in Manachiḥṛ's speedy death. Antiochus, having now reduced the country to order and seated *Khosṛov* firmly on the throne, collected the tribute due to the emperor and withdrew from Armenia.

Khosṛov sometime after this, in order to protect himself from rebellions instigated by Sapor, agreed to pay him a tribute every year. The country now enjoyed some years of peace, during which *Khosṛov* built a city called Dovin or Blouṛ, in the district of Bagṛevan, and made it his capital. By his orders Vachhê planted two royal forests or parks for him, one extending from the fort called Garni to the valley of the Medsamôṛ and thence to Dovin, and another somewhat further south. Both were well stocked with game, to enable *Khosṛov* to indulge in the chase, a favourite pastime of all the Arsacide monarchs.

It was while *Khosṛov* was engaged in these affairs that Sanatṛouk at last began the attack on Armenia for which he had made such extensive preparations. With an immense host of Huns, Gongarians, Sarmatians and other northern tribes, and assured of assistance from Sapor, Sanatṛouk crossed the river Kouṛ, and spread devastation and bloodshed through the country. His host is said to have been so numerous that the only way in which its leaders could estimate the numbers of their forces was by issuing orders that each man should cast a stone on the ground when passing the places where roads from different directions met. The immense piles of stones thus formed gave some idea of the size of the horde that had passed. Wandering in different directions through the country, pillaging and murdering as they advanced, they gradually neared their appointed rendezvous near the city of Vagharshapat. Unable to resist the invaders, *Khosṛov* and Vṛthanês fled for refuge to the fortress of Daṛevnikh, in the district of Kovg. Vachhê was then absent on a journey ; but on his return he, in concert with Bagṛat Bagṛatouni, Meḥoundak Rshtouni, Gaṛegin Rshtouni, Vaḥan Amatouni, and Vaṛaz, fell on a large party of the northern tribes at a mountain called Tsou Klou*kh* or ' Bull's Head,' and taking them by surprise in the early morning, almost annihilated them. Then advancing to Vagharshapat, the Armenian army assailed Sanatṛouk and his Persian allies at that city, defeated them with great slaughter, and recovered the city. The enemy fled to the fortress of Hôshak or Ôshakan, not far from Vagharshapat. Another great victory finally relieved Armenia of these invaders (a. d. 350). Sanatṛouk himself fell, and his head was brought to *Khosṛov,* who shed tears over the fate of his Arsacide kinsman and enemy. The king visited the battle-field in company with Vṛthanês, and seeing that it was impossible to bury the enormous mass of the slain, commanded that rocks should be heaped over them, to prevent a pestilence. After this great victory, *Khosṛov* ceased to pay tribute to the Persians. The rest of his life was spent peacefully, and he died in a.d. 352, leaving his kingdom to his son Tiṛan II.

Tiṛan was both weak and vicious. A man less fitted to guide the helm of state at such a critical period could hardly have been found. But Vṛthanês, calling a council of nobles, succeeded in getting a resolution passed directing him to go with Tiṛan to Constantinople, in order to obtain for him from the emperor recognition as king and the ensigns of royalty. Meanwhile the defence of the country was entrusted to Aṛshaviṛ Kamsaṛakan.

Sapor considered this a favourable opportunity to wrest Armenia from the Romans. He proclaimed his own brother Neṛseḥ king, and sent him to Armenia with a large army. A battle was fought in the plain of Mrough, where Aṛshaviṛ completely defeated the Persians and drove Neṛseḥ out of Armenia. On Tiṛan's return, however, the latter, being anxious for peace, agreed to pay Sapor the same amount of tribute that he already paid to Constantius. By this means he secured the assistance of the Persians in repelling another inroad of the northern tribes (a. d. 359). Meanwhile, being thus at peace for a time, Tiṛan was able to give himself up to vice and luxury, though the awe in which Vṛthanês kept him made him conceal his evil habits as much as possible from the Katholicos.

Vṛthanês died in a.d. 355, and was succeeded in the patriarchal dignity by his only remaining son. Housik, who was consecrated Katholicos in a. d. 356, and whose life and conduct proved him a worthy successor to those who had preceded him in that high office. His sons, Pap and Athanaginês, were a source of much grief to him, but his hopes were centred in Neṛsês, a son of the latter, who would, he believed, fulfill the prophecy which had been made years before. The Katholicos therefore sent the child to Caesarea, to be out of the way of his father's evil influence, and to be educated in the learning of the Greeks. When older, Neṛsês went to finish his education at Constantinople, where he married a daughter of a nobleman named Aspianês.

The war which the Emperor Julian the Apostate waged with Sapor II made Tiṛan's position as the ally and tributary of *both* empires a very uncomfortable one. Sapor's capital was Ctesiphon. Julian marched an army into Mesopotamia and endeavoured to cross the Euphrates, in order to invade the Persian territories in that direction. The Persians, however, had destroyed the bridge over the river, and an army was stationed there to oppose his crossing. Julian then wrote to Tiṛan, demanding aid from the latter (a. d. 362). Tiṛan was obliged to break his treaty with Sapor by sending a force to drive away that of the Persians opposed to Julian on the Euphrates, and to rebuild the bridge. He, however, refused to march with the emperor against Sapor, on the plea that he, as a Christian, could not serve under an idolatrous banner. Julian compelled him to place at his disposal the Armenian force stationed to guard the southern parts of the country, and to send his third son, Tiridatês, with the wife and children of the latter, to Constanti-nople as hostages for his good behaviour. Julian also sent his own picture to Tiṛan, commanding him to hang it up in the church at the capital, as a sign that Armenia was tributary to the Roman empire. In this Julian revived a custom of the old heathen emperors. Tiṛan ordered the picture to be placed in the royal chapel in the canton of Dsophkh. But the Katholicos remonstrated against such desecration, and, finding his protests unavailing, tore the picture from its place and trampled it underfoot. Tiṛan, enraged at this, and already cherishing a grudge against the Katholicos for family reasons, ordered him to be scourged. He was accordingly flogged to death, thus adding another to the long roll of Armenian martyrs.

An aged Syrian, Daniel, a disciple of Gregory the Illuminator, who had consecrated him Chorepiscopus, and who resided in a monastery in the canton of Taṛôn, was chosen by the king and the nobles to succeed Housik in the office of Katholicos. The brave old man came to court, and boldly reproached the king for the murder of Housik and his unworthy conduct in obeying Julian's order. Enraged at this, Tiṛan ordered him to be strangled. The office was then offered to Pap and Athanaginês, who both declined it. They were compelled to be ordained deacons, but were destroyed by fire from heaven the same year because of their evil lives (a. d. 362).

The Armenian force which was serving under Julian's orders now deserted his standard and, with their commander Zauṛa, returned to Armenia. Incensed at this, Julian sent orders to Tiṛan to put Zauṛa to death, and he and his whole family were accordingly exterminated. Julian's own death soon followed. Jovian, who was elected emperor by the army, concluded a peace with Sapor and withdrew from Persia, but died on his homeward march.

Sapor then marched into Armenia, resolved to punish Tiṛan for his treachery to himself. Summoning the Armenian monarch to meet him at his camp near the village of Aṛdsiv, in the canton of Apaḥounikh, Sapor received him with honour ; but when he had him in his power, he seized him and put out both his eyes, and then sent him as prisoner to the town of Kovash, at the foot of Mount Aṛagds (a.d. 362). So speedily did Tiṛan's punishment follow his guilt.

The Persian monarch appointed Tiṛan's son, Aṛshak II, King of Armenia. But he acted as though he meant to be himself the real ruler of the country and render Aṛshak a mere puppet in his hands. Taking some of the leading nobles with him as hostages for the rest, Sapor marched into Bithynia, to attack the Romans in their own territory. He did not, however, meet with the success he expected there, and was forced to retire to his own country. He shortly afterwards invaded Mesopotamia, but there concluded a treaty with Valentinianus I, which set him free to inflict terrible persecution on the numerous Christians who were then to be found in Persia. He did not, however, consider himself sufficiently strong to venture to extend the same treatment to those of Armenia, though the latter country was now, for a time at least, under his authority.

On the murder of Daniel the Katholicos in a.d. 362, a monk named Pharneṛseh or Pharên, from the monastery of St. John the Baptist in Taṛôn, was appointed to succeed him, as the nobles assured Tiṛan that it was absolutely necessary to find someone to fill the office, since the people had such a veneration for the patriarchate that, unless one were appointed, there would be danger of a rebellion. Neṛsês, the representative of Gregory's house, would most probably have been chosen to occupy the position, which might almost be said to be hereditary in the family of the Illuminator, had he then been in Armenia. But he was resident at Constantinople, and it may well be believed that the king was in no hurry to urge the return and appointment to the archiepiscopal dignity of a man likely to be both strong and good, and therefore bound to oppose him in his evil conduct. Pharên occupied the patriarchal throne for only about two years, dying in a. d. 364. On his death it was resolved to elect Neṛsês as Katholicos, though he was still absent from the country. This was done, and the nobles sent an urgent message to him, begging him to return to his fatherland. Neṛsês acceded to their desire, and was consecrated at Caesarea on his way to Armenia.

When he reached his native land, the nobles and people received him with great gladness (a.d. 365). He immediately set about the reformation of abuses which had crept into the Church during recent times, endeavouring very successfully to restore the strict and healthy discipline which had been maintained under his great progenitor, and to abolish the laxity of morals and general disorganization which had of late prevailed. He also introduced many ecclesiastical improvements which he had seen in Constantinople. By the king's permission he called a great council or synod of all the bishops and many leading nobles, which met at Ashtishat in a. d. 365, the main object of which was the correction of abuses in the Church. The chief of these which were condemned at the council were: (1) marriages contracted between near relatives, among the nobles more especially, with the object of retaining property in the family ; (2)the practice of indulging in excessive mourning for the dead, and in conduct unworthy of Christians ; (3) the habit of expelling from the towns and villages all lepers and persons suffering from infectious diseases. Such unfortunates, besides the lame, the blind, and hopeless incurables, were often left unaided to die of starvation. To put a stop to the latter practice, Neṛsês was successful in getting hospitals and suitable asylums built in every canton for the reception of these unfortunates. He also erected orphanages and places where widows and the poor might receive help, and succeeded in having taxes levied for their endowment. In certain places where they were most needed, he also built rest houses for travellers.

Aṛshak proved as little fitted to rule as his father Tiṛan had been. His weakness, viciousness, cruelty and cowardice very soon reduced the country to a state of anarchy. It was largely owing to the great influence exercised over the nobility and people by Neṛsês the Katholicos, deservedly entitled the Great, that things were not even worse. We have seen some of the improvements he introduced in religious and social matters. In politics his influence was also great, and was always exercised with the noblest motives and for the good of his country and people. A good instance of this is afforded by the following incident :—Valentinianus, the emperor, sent legates to Aṛshak's court to invite him to free himself from his degrading subjection to the Persians and to assume towards the Byzantine empire the same relations and position which the Kings of Armenia before him had held for some generations, in fact, from Nero's time, with but few interruptions. Aṛshak treated these ambassadors with dishonour, and as a natural consequence excited the anger of Valentinianus, who in revenge put to death Tiridatês, one of Aṛshak's brothers, who had been sent to Constantinople as a hostage by Julian. When this news reached Armenia, and it seemed likely that a Byzantine army would soon invade the country, Aṛshak trembled, and sent Neṛsês to the imperial court to appease the emperor. Neṛsês, having studied at both Caesarea and Constantinople, was famed for his eloquence and perfect command of Greek, and being allied by marriage with a noble family at Constantinople, was able to enlist some of the emperor's court to support his plea that the latter would overlook Aṛshak's offence and be reconciled. Neṛsês succeeded so com-pletely in his embassy that he not only prevented war, but also secured the release of Gnêl, son of Aṛshak 's brother Tiridatês, and the other Armenian hostages who had hitherto been detained at Constantinople. In order still further to cement the friendship formed between the emperor and the Armenian monarch, a marriage was celebrated between the latter and a maiden of the imperial house named Olympias, and Aṛshak was recognized as a tributary ally of the empire.

On learning this, Sapor prepared to march an army into Armenia in order to punish Aṛshak for his defection. To prevent this, Aṛshak sent ambassadors to Ctesiphon, begging for restoration to favour. Sapor was willing to grant forgiveness on condition that Aṛshak should break off his alliance with Valentini-anus and aid the Persians in a war with the Byzantine empire. Aṛshak, with a weakling's vacillation, endeavoured to please both parties, but succeeded only in incurring the distrust of both. He was unable to prevent Sapor from marching through Armenia to attack the Roman dominions in Asia Minor, but commanded Ardovk, ruler of Siunikh, to refuse the Persian monarch permission to enter the city of Tigranocerta. Sapor passed on, but threatened to exact a terrible vengeance. Accordingly, on his return, he carried the city by storm, utterly destroyed it, and carried off to Persia as captives all its citizens who did not perish in the massacre.

Valentinianus, learning of Aṛshak's dealings with the Persians, sent an army under the brave Theodosius to invade Armenia. To avert this, Neṛsês was again sent as an ambassador to Constantinople. He arrived shortly after Valentinianus' death (a.d. 375), and failed to influence Valens, who was an Arian. Valens refused the Katholicos an audience, and banished him to an island.

Before this, however, matters had reached a crisis in Armenia. Aṛshak's cruelty and incapacity had given his nobles just cause for offence, but a great crime which he now committed compelled them to take up arms against him. Aṛshak 's nephew, Gnêl, on his return from Constantinople, had gone to live at Kovash with his blind grandfather, the deposed King Tiṛan, with whom he became a great favourite. He married Pharantzem, daughter of Ardovk, and was given great wealth by Tiṛan. Besides this, Gnêl gained great popularity, and thereby excited Aṛshak's jealousy, who banished him to a place called Shaḥapivan. Tiṛan severely reproved Aṛshak for his in-justice, and was shortly after strangled by his orders. Aṛshak then got Gnêl murdered in the chase, by a pretended accident, and took his wife as a concubine. The latter, jealous of the superior position occupied by Queen Olympias, bribed a priest named Mṛjiunik to poison the queen, which he did by mingling poison in the cup at Holy Communion. Pharantzem thereupon became queen ; and Neṛsês, grieved by the occurrence of such crimes, quitted the court.

Aṛshak, true to the traditions of his family, resolved to build a city to serve as his memorial. He founded one at the foot of Mount Masis (Ararat), and named it Aṛshakavan, or Aṛshak's town. In order to people it, he made it a sanctuary for all criminals and fugitives from justice, including runaway serfs. It soon became full of most undesirable characters, who made themselves a nuisance to the country at large. This enraged the nobles and proved the immediate cause of the revolt which soon after broke out. The Persian King Sapor had then just finished the capture of Tigranocerta. The nobles appealed to him for help. He granted their request, and they with his assistance stormed Aṛshakavan and razed it to the ground, putting all the inhabitants to the sword except the little boys, whom they divided among themselves as slaves. But Neṛsês the Katholicos, hearing of this, arrived in time to recover them, and had them brought up in the orphanages which he had founded.

Sapor and the Armenian nobles easily routed any troops which Aṛshak was able to bring into the field, and Aṛshak himself was obliged to flee for refuge to Georgia. Meanwhile Sapor treated Armenia like a conquered country. He captured the fortress of Ani, which still held out for the king, carried off the royal treasures which were kept there, and even dug up the bones of earlier Kings of Armenia, whose tombs were there, and carried them with him on his return to Persia. But the Armenian nobles attacked the detachment which guarded these strange spoils, and recovering them, interred them at the town of Aghtskh.

Meanwhile Aṛshak had collected an army and returned to recover his throne. The leader of the rebels was Neṛsês Kamsaṛakan. The civil war lasted for about two years. At last, after great slaughter on both sides, Neṛsês the Katholicos, with great difficulty, succeeded in effecting a reconciliation between the two contending parties. This was in some measure brought about by the news that the Byzantine emperor had resolved to send an army against Armenia. Having succeeded in securing peace within the country itself, Neṛsês now went to Constantinople to avert the emperor's wrath, taking with him as a hostage Aṛshak's son Pap. We have already learnt the unfavourable reception he received (a.d. 375).

Two only of the greater nobles, Meṛouzhan Aṛdsṛounî and Vaḥan Mamikoni, had refused to be reconciled to Aṛshak, and, distrusting his promises, fled to Persia. Their wisdom was evident in the sequel. For Aṛshak, taking advantage of Neṛsês the Katholicos' absence, shamefully broke all his agreements and took vengeance upon many of the nobles for their rebellion. He put many of them to death on various pretexts and confiscated their property. His wrath fell more especially upon the whole family of the Kamsaṛakans. He massacred every member of that family, with the exception of one son, Spandaṛat, who succeeded in making his escape to the Byzantine court. When the serfs belonging to that unhappy house showed their devotion by burying the bodies of their murdered masters, the king caused them to be hanged, as a reward for their courage and fidelity.

The situation had now become unbearable, and the nobles again rose in revolt and asked assistance from Sapor. The latter was only too glad to embrace the opportunity of making himself master of Armenia. He sent a large army into the country, under the command of a Parthian noble named Alanozan. Aṛshak, unable to resist, tried to corrupt the latter by offering him a large bribe. In this, however, he failed, and was obliged to surrender to Sapor, who at first treated him with great kindness. But when the nobles found that Sapor wished to remove Queen Pharantzem and their own wives as hostages to Persia, they rebelled and attacked the Persian forces. Failing in their attempt to expel them from the country, they themselves with their families fled to Valens' court. Pharantzem collected what treasure she could, and fortified herself in the fort of Aṛtageṛs, expecting the return of her son Pap from Constantinople. Sapor thereupon threw Aṛshak into chains, and imprisoned him in the fortress of Anhoush in Khuzistân. He entrusted the renegade nobles Meṛouzhan and Vahan with an army, and sent them back to effect the subjugation of Armenia (a.d. 378), promising the crown to the former and a great reward to the latter, if they succeeded in doing the work so effectually as to force the people to renounce Christianity and embrace the Magian faith. These nobles besieged and captured the fortress of Aṛtageṛs, and sent the queen to Syria, where she met the fate she had by her crimes so richly deserved, being put to death there by being impaled.

When news of all this reached Aṛshak in his prison, he despaired of recovering his power, and falling a prey to the tortures of remorse, committed suicide (a.d. 382).

CHAPTER XII

THE LAST YEARS OF THE ARSACIDE DYNASTY

' Si l'Eglise chrétienne n'avait pas existé, le monde entier aurait été livré à la pure force matérielle. L'Église seule exerçait un pouvoir moral.'—Guizot, *Hist, de la Civilisation en Europe,* Lect. ii.

Armenia now seemed to lie completely at the mercy of the Persians. Her king had died in a Persian prison, her leading nobles were refugees in the Byzantine empire, her treasures had been plundered, her army dispersed, her patriarch was in exile, and a large Persian force, under the command of a rene-gade noble, held the country for Sapor. The opportunity seemed favourable for incorporating the country with the Persian empire, and so strengthening the latter very materially and depriving the Byzantines of a useful ally. But Sapor felt that, in order to separate Armenia forever from the Roman alliance, it was necessary to sever the ties of religion and language which bound the Armenians to that empire. The fact that Christianity had now become the religion of both the Roman empire and of the Armenian nation bound the latter country to the court of Constantinople, while rendering the people hostile to the Persians, who were zealous for the Magian religion and bitter enemies of the Gospel. It was therefore necessary, for political as well as for religious reasons, to induce the Armenians to embrace Magianism. In order to render their conversion easier, all communication with Constantinople must be made impossible. Meṛouzhan, who had married Sapor's sister Ormazddoukht, encouraged to hope for the crown of Armenia if he succeeded in subduing the country, resolved, in order to do this more effectually, to proscribe Greek learning in Armenia. He therefore burnt all the Greek books he could find, including all copies of the Holy Scriptures and religious works which fell into his hands, and forbade any to study that language. He began to persecute the leading clergy, putting many of them to death, and sending others as prisoners to Persia, on the pretext that they had not paid the tax imposed on them. The study of the Persian language was encouraged in the country, and every inducement was held out to the nobles and leading men to become converts to Magianism. As there existed at that time no Armenian version of the Bible, the services being conducted in Greek or Syriac , the task of weaning the people from the Gospel by these and similar measures seemed by no means hopeless. Meṛouzhan did not disdain to capture and imprison the wives of the nobles who had fled alone to Constantinople, hoping in this way to compel their husbands to return and submit to his authority.

Neṛsês the Great, having been recalled from exile, was then at Constantinople at the court of Theodosius I.

Deeply stirred by the miseries of his country, he exerted all his influence and eloquence with the object of inducing the emperor to espouse the cause of Armenia. He succeeded in having Pap, Aṛshak's son and heir, appointed king, and in getting a Byzantine army under the command of Terentianus sent with him to restore that prince to his inheritance (a. d. 382). The Katholicos himself and the refugee nobles returned with the young king. Meṛouzhan found himself unable to cope with Terentianus. He accordingly fled to Persia, having first commanded the officers in charge of the various forts in which the wives of the nobles were confined to hang these hapless ladies on the walls before their returning husbands' eyes.

Sapor assembled a large army and sent Meṛouzhan back to expel the Byzantine forces, which had then received reinforcements under Count Addê. A great and decisive battle was fought in the plain of Tziṛav, near Mount Niphatês. The Katholicos and the king watched its progress with great anxiety, knowing that the fate of the country depended upon its issue. Like another Moses, Neṛsês uplifted his hands in prayer for his people. We are informed that thereupon a strong wind arose, which blew the Persian arrows and darts back upon themselves, while a cloud obscured the sun and prevented its rays from dazzling the Armenians and encouraging its Persian worshippers. The victory remained with the Armenians, while the Persians were utterly routed, and their leaders slain. Vahan Mamikoni fell by the hand of his own son Samuel. Meṛouzhan fled for his life, but

was pursued and overtaken by Smbat Bagṛatouni, who placed on his head in mockery a red-hot iron circlet, formed from a spit or dart, crying, ' With this do I crown thee, Meṛouzhan, as thou wishest to be King of Armenia.

Pap now ascended the throne, and dismissed to their homes with rich rewards the Byzantine forces to whom he owed his restoration. He reorganized the Armenian army, placing at its head Moushegh Mamikonean, who had shown great bravery in the late battle. The king and the nobles vowed in Neṛsês' presence that they would be faithful to God and to one another. Pap restored to the nobles the estates which Aṛshak had confiscated, and for a short time all went well. But the king soon fell into the ways of his father. Neṛsês earnestly remonstrated with him, but in vain. Wearying of his faithful warnings, Pap secretly poisoned him (a.d. 383).

But punishment soon followed upon this crime ; for when Pap, taking advantage of internal troubles within the empire, endeavoured to free himself from Byzantine control and ally himself with Persia, he was seized by Terentianus and carried off to Byzantium, where he was beheaded by the orders of Theodosius (a.d. 388). Pap's vices were so horrible that Faustus Byzantinus informs us that it was generally believed he was possessed of the devil even from his birth.

Theodosius appointed Pap's brother's son, Vaṛazdat, King of Armenia, as Pap's own sons were too young to reign (a.d. 391). Vaṛazdat had some years previously fled to Constantinople, where, by his courage and ability, he had made himself famous, and had gained the emperor's favour. It was believed that his long residence in the Byzantine empire had made him a sincere friend, and that he might be trusted to maintain the alliance between Armenia and that empire. But shortly after his return to Armenia, Vaṛazdat endeavoured to enter into an agreement with Sapor, hoping thus to free himself from the suzerainty of Byzantium, which he found very irksome. The plot was discovered, and, to avoid being carried prisoner to Constantinople, Vaṛazdat went there of his own accord, hoping to clear himself of the charge brought against him. But on his arrival the emperor refused him an audience, and banished him to distant Thulê. (a.d. 394).

Theodosius then appointed Pap's two sons, Aṛshak III and Vagharṣhak II, to rule Armenia jointly, hoping that one would be a check upon the other, and that all danger of treasonable intriguing with the court of Ctesiphon would be prevented. Aṛshak set up his court at Dovin, while Vagharṣhak chose Eṛiza as his capital (a.d. 394), both being supported by a Byzantine army. But Vagharṣhak died before he had reigned for a single year.

In the following year (Jan. 395 a.d.) the Emperor Theodosius himself died, leaving the empire of the West to his son Honorius, and that of the East to Arcadius. The latter was a mere puppet in the hands of his courtiers. In order to put an end to the hostilities between the Persian and the Byzantine empires that had now lasted for so many years with no decided advantage to either party, Arcadius and Sapor entered into an agreement to divide Armenia and Mesopotamia between them. The eastern and larger portion of Armenia fell to Sapor. Aṛshak, who on his brother's death had for a time reigned over the whole country, continued to rule the portion of the country which had now become part of the Byzantine dominions. Sapor appointed an Arsacide chief named *Khosṛov* to rule over the rest of the country (a.d. 396), with the title of *Khosṛov* III. Many of the Armenian nobles had left their estates and gone to Aṛshak's court rather than submit to a heathen sovereign. Sapor now proclaimed his intention of confiscating their estates if they did not return and submit to *Khosṛov*. The result was that most of them did so, and Aṛshak was left with only those few of the nobles whose estates lay within the Byzantine territory, and those who were closely re-lated to himself or who had reason to fear Sapor's personal ill-will.

A war broke out soon after between Aṛshak and *Khosṛov* in the following manner. Saḥak Bagṛatouni, father-in-law of Vagharṣhak II, having suffered family dishonour from Aṛshak, left his court and betook himself to Persian Armenia, where he was honourably received by *Khosṛov,* who appointed him general of his army, and, in lieu of his estates which Aṛshak had confiscated, conferred on him some of those which had belonged to certain of Aṛshak's partisans. Shortly after this Saḥak was sent to subdue some marauders

who, from their stronghold in the mountains of Taikh, plundered both kingdoms with the strictest impar-tiality. Saḥak slaughtered many of them, and drove the rest into the canton of Mananagh. Pursuing them into that canton, he there met with Samuel Mamikonean, who was in command of Aṛshak's forces, and who was pursuing some nobles that, apparently at Saḥak's instigation, had seized Aṛshak's treasures, and were carrying them off to *Khosṛov*. A battle ensued, but Saḥak seems to have got the better of Samuel, for he succeeded in carrying the treasures and their plunderers in safety to *Khosṛov*'s court. The latter sent part of the treasure to Sapor and rewarded the robbers. When Aṛshak's demand for their restoration was refused, war ensued. A battle was fought in the plain of Eṛevel, in the canton of Vanand. In this battle Aṛshak's army was defeated, and the king was in imminent danger of capture, while his general, Dara Siuni, fell on the field. Aṛshak did not long survive his defeat, dying in a.d. 399.

The Byzantine court appointed a brave Armenian noble, Gazavon Kamsaṛakan, as commander-in-chief of their forces in the western part of Armenia, and ruled the country for a time by sending a Greek count as governor, instead of nominating another king, for Aṛshak had died childless. The Armenian nobles in Byzantine territory, however, did not approve of this. They therefore intrigued with *Khosṛov* through Gazavon, and agreed to recognize him as their king, on condition of his restoring to them their forfeited estates within his territory, and undertaking to protect from the Byzantine governor those whose property lay within the Byzantine part of Armenia. In this way *Khosṛov* gained the support of all but one of the nobles. He then sent an embassy to Constantinople, proposing that he should be recognized as king of the whole of Armenia, promising, in that case, faithfully to pay to the Byzantine court as tribute the same annual sum that was now collected from their portion of Armenia in the form of taxes. Arcadius accepted this proposal, and *Khosṛov* became monarch of both divisions of the country.

Khosṛov's dealings with the Byzantine court readily lent themselves to misconstruction. Some Armenian nobles who cherished ill-will against him circulated at Ctesiphon the report that he had resolved, when a suitable opportunity should occur, to shake off his allegiance to Sapor and to ally himself with Arcadius. This rumour seemed to receive additional confirmation when *Khosṛov*, without consulting Sapor, appointed Saḥak, surnamed the Parthian, only son of Neṛsês the Great, to the high office of Katholicos of Armenia. Saḥak, like all the descendants of Gregory the Illuminator, was regarded as a warm partisan of Byzantium and as irreconcilably hostile to Persia. Thereupon Sapor sent a very decided warning to *Khosṛov*, threatening to dethrone him if he showed any further inclination to forget what he owed to the court of Ctesiphon. The natural result of such a threat was to throw *Khosṛov* into the arms of the Byzantines. He made a new agreement with Arcadius, by which he agreed to place the whole kingdom under the suzerainty of Byzantium, on condition that Arcadius sent him troops to protect him from the wrath of the dread Persian monarch.

But before such help could reach him the blow fell. Sapor sent his son Ardashîr into Armenia at the head of an army. *Khosṛov*, in despair, endeavoured to get assistance from the northern tribes, but in this too he was disappointed. He was compelled to surrender himself to Ardashîr, who sent him in chains to Persia, where he was confined in the fortress of Anhoush (a.d. 400). Ardashîr placed on the vacant throne Vramshapouḥ, *Khosṛov*'s brother.

Vramshapouḥ was a wise and virtuous prince, and during his reign of twenty-one years he not only proved faithful to his Persian suzerain, but also strove to live for the highest interests of his country. His reign is forever memorable for the fact that during it the present Armenian alphabet was invented by Mesṛop, and the beginning of the extant literature of Armenia was made. The details of this most important work we reserve for the last chapter but one of the present volume. The king himself entered heartily into the scheme for providing Armenia with an indigenous literature, as well as into every other plan which seemed likely to result in real benefit to the nation at large. The peace and quietness that prevailed in Armenia during Vramshapouḥ's comparatively long reign afforded Saḥak and Mesṛop time to develop their plans and see them approach complete realization before the beginning of the troubles which, a

few years later, threatened to involve both Church and State in one common ruin.
Saḥak was a worthy successor of the noble men, his ancestors, who had before him held the office of Katholicos. But his ability and influence were at first rather a hindrance than a help to him, for on *Khosṛov*'s fall he was for a time deprived of the patriarchate by the Persian monarch. However, he was soon restored to it, and devoted himself to the discharge of the multiplex duties of his office, gaining great influence not only in Armenia, but in Persia also. Saḥak gave his only daughter, Saḥakanoish, in marriage to a leading noble, Ḥamazasp Mamikonean, and, after the death of Saḥak Bagṛatouni, he several times requested *Khosṛov* to make Ḥamazasp general of his forces. *Khosṛov* refused to do so ; but when the same request was made to Vramshapouḥ, the latter stated that he would readily grant it, provided the consent of Ardashîr, the new King of Persia, could be obtained. Saḥak then started for the Persian court, provided with a letter of recommendation from Vramshapouḥ. Ardashîr received him with honour, and granted his request.
Vramshapouḥ died in a.d. 421, leaving a son hardly ten years of age. As the country was in no fitting state to be ruled by a child, the nobles met in council, and sent Saḥak to the Persian court to entreat King Yezdigird I to release *Khosṛov* III, who still lingered in his prison, and to restore him to the throne. Yezdigird, out of respect for the memory of Vramshapouḥ, granted their request, and *Khosṛov* again ascended the throne. But he died the same year (a.d. 421).
Yezdigird now resolved to render Armenia an integral part of the Persian empire. He therefore declined to appoint another Arsacide king, but sent his own son Sapor to Armenia with the royal title. Ḥamazasp, the general of the Armenian army, was now dead, and for a time the Armenians had no recognized leader, and were unable to oppose Sapor's accession to the throne. But four years later Sapor was recalled to Persia by the news of his father's serious illness. He left the government of Armenia in the hands of a viceroy, with orders to the latter to capture the principal nobles and send them prisoners to Persia.
When an attempt was made to carry out this order, the nobles rose in rebellion under Neṛsês Chichṛakatsi, and falling unexpectedly upon the Persian troops in their country, routed them with great slaughter. But, being unable to oppose the Persian army which King Vram (Varanês, Bahrâm) V sent against them, they dispersed to their castles, from which they kept up a desultory warfare. The country was filled with bloodshed and desolation.
During this time the Katholicos paid a visit to the portion of Armenia which belonged to the Byzantine empire. There he found that the people were greatly oppressed by their Byzantine governors, who utterly refused to receive Saḥak or show him any respect. The Katholicos therefore sent Mesṛop and his own grandson Vaṛdan Mamikonean to the court of Theodosius II, to request that his authority as Katholicos should be fully recognized in the Byzantine portion of the country, and that he should be permitted to open schools there for the instruction of the people in their own language. Theodosius granted this request, and Saḥak was thus enabled to introduce the newly invented Armenian alphabet into that province also.
The Persian monarch had meanwhile learnt by experience the impossibility of ruling Armenia unless by conciliating the nobles. He therefore conferred with them regarding the government of the country, and at their request appointed Aṛtashês, son of Vramshapouḥ, king. The latter was at that time only about fifteen years of age (A. d. 426). But he soon rendered himself an object of hatred and contempt to everyone, to such an extent that the nobles proposed to Saḥak that they should ask Vram to dethrone him and appoint a Persian governor to rule the country instead. Saḥak opposed this plan with all his might, foreseeing that it would lead to the destruction of the country, the persecution of the Church, and loss of every semblance of liberty. The nobles urged that it would be better to be ruled by a wise and just Persian governor than by a vicious and dissipated lad like Aṛtashês. The Katholicos replied, ' God forbid that I should exchange this my sickly sheep for a healthy wild beast, whose very soundness would cause us misery.' The nobles thereupon sent a petition to Vram, begging him to depose both Aṛtashês and Saḥak from their respective offices. The Persian monarch summoned them both to his presence, and, without giving them any chance of defending themselves, deposed them and ordered them to remain in Persia. In their stead, Vram appointed a Persian official with the title of *Marzbân,* or 'Warden of the Marshes,' to rule the country, and made an Armenian priest named Mouṛmak Katholicos (a.d. 432).
Thus fell in Armenia the last prince of the Arsacide dynasty, which had ruled the country with varying fortune for five hundred and eighty-two years. At the same time the office of Katholicos, which had, with but slight interruption, been hereditary in the family of Gregory the Illuminator for one hundred and thirty years, passed for ever into other hands.

CHAPTER XIII

MESROP, SAHAK, AND THE ARMENIAN BIBLE

'Ethê Hayĕ, ain boloṛ phothoṛikneṛi tak, oṛ skseal ḥingeṛoṛd daṛouts ekel en Phokhṛ Asiayi ev manavand the Ḥayastani veṛah, paḥpanouel é oṛpês mi inkhnishkhan khṛistoneah azg, aid banĕ ais arantzin, azgayin lezouin haṛmaṛetsṛads nshanagṛeṛi ptoughn ê.'—Stephen Nazaṛeants in *Hiusisaphail.*

'If, during all those tempests which, beginning from the fifth century, have come upon Asia Minor and especially upon Armenia, the Armenian has been preserved as an independent Christian nation, that circumstance is the fruit of these peculiar written characters, adapted to the national language.'

The great work of the conversion of Armenia to the Christian faith, begun by Gregory the Illuminator, had been left unfinished in at least one very important respect. Gregory had seen the desirability of ren-dering the Church of Armenia as soon as possible independent of foreign missionaries, and had accord-ingly established schools for the education of the people and for the training of indigenous clergy. But, as there was no Armenian literature worthy of the name at that time extant, and as no suitable alphabet capable of properly representing the sounds of the language had as yet been invented, he had not attempted to translate into the language of the people the Scriptures and the, service-books used in divine worship. Greek and Syriac were carefully taught in the numerous schools established throughout the country by Gregory, and it became the practice to read the Scriptures either in Greek or in Syriac—whichever language the officiating minister knew best —and to explain to the people in the vernacular the meaning of what they heard.

This was evidently only a temporary measure, and it worked fairly well for a time. The schools turned out a considerable number of preachers and teachers able to expound to the people the meaning of the Greek and Syriac texts, and so the pressing need of an Armenian version was not so much felt. But during the troubles which followed on Tiridatês' death the schools gradually lost both teachers and pupils. The new generation of clergy could indeed read the sacred texts, but they understood them less and less. During the persecution under Meṛouzhan the study of Greek was. as we have already seen, entirely prohibited, and all Greek books which were found in the country were ruthlessly burnt. No serious attempt seems to have been made to interfere with the use of Syriac in worship ; but the congrega-tions accustomed to worship in Greek found their clergy in most instances quite unable to interpret to them the Syriac Scriptures. The result was, as ancient Armenian historians inform us, that the people left their churches uncomforted by the Words of Life, which they had heard with their outward ears, but which they had been utterly unable to understand. Day by day this state of things grew worse and worse. Ignorance of the doctrines of Christianity spread rapidly, and there was great danger that the people would in consequence either lapse into their old heathen practices or at least be unable to withstand the efforts for their conversion to Magianism made by the Persian court. This was the state of affairs which led to the invention of the Armenian alphabet still (with slight modifications) in use, and to the ultimate translation of the Holy Scriptures into that language.

This great work was accomplished by the Katholicos Saḥak in some measure, but more particularly by his famous associate and fellow-labourer Mesṛop Mashtots.

Mesṛop was born in the village of Ḥatsik, in the canton of Taṛôn. His father Vaṛdan taught him a little Greek, and when still young he became a pupil of Neṛsês the Great, under whom he soon mastered Greek, Syriac and Persian. When he grew up he became for a time one of the court scribes, and found his knowledge useful in that capacity, for at that time the letters and edicts of Armenian kings were generally published in all three languages. He devoted himself to all secular studies, especially Greek, and became much respected by small and great, as his friend and biographer Koriun informs us. Wearying, however, of secular work, Mesṛop soon left the court, and retiring to a hermitage with a few disciples, devoted himself to the practice of austerities and the preaching of the Gospel. He went especially to preach in those parts of the country, such as the canton of Goghthn, where heathen practices still prevailed among the people, having never entirely ceased. With the favour and assistance of Sabith or Sabath, the chief of the district, Mesṛop and his disciples were enabled to work a great reformation there, and the gods are said to have fled in a bodily form from them and to have retired into Media. Being well acquainted with Syriac, Mesṛop himself did not find it a very difficult task to translate orally to the people the passages of Scripture read to them in church, but the work was far more difficult for his disciples to perform. During the time that he spent in itinerating and preaching the Gospel in different parts of the country Mesṛop felt more and more how absolutely necessary it was for the people to have the Scriptures translated into and published in their native tongue. But before this could be done it was necessary to invent an alphabet suited to the genius of the language. Owing to the number of sounds which Armenian possesses, neither the Greek nor the Syrian, nor even the Pahlavî, alphabet was at all suitable to write Armenian in. To the task of devising a really suitable alphabet and of having an Armenian version of the Scriptures made, Mesṛop now determined to devote all his energies.

Accordingly, leaving his hermitage, Mesṛop came to Saḥak the Katholicos and told him his plans (a. d. 397). This wise and good man showed the greatest possible interest in them, and gave Mesṛop every encouragement to continue the efforts he had already begun to make with the object of devising an Armenian alphabet. Mesṛop renewed his efforts, with fervent prayer to God for guidance.

About this time King Vramshapouḥ, who, at the request of the King of Persia, had visited Mesopotamia in order to arrange a dispute which had arisen in that country between himself and the Byzantine court, met a Syrian presbyter named Abel, who informed him that a learned and pious Syrian bishop, Daniel by name, had by him an alphabet which had formerly been used for writing Armenian. The king took no notice of this statement at the time, but did not forget it. By Mesṛop's advice, Saḥak got Vramshapouḥ to call a great council of the nobility and of the bishops and principal clergy of his realm, in order to decide what steps should be taken with the object of obtain-ing an Armenian literature. This council met at Vagharṣhapat in a.d. 402. The king himself was present and mentioned what he had heard about an Armenian alphabet. The council took the matter up most warmly, and entreated the king to send messengers to Mesopotamia at once to visit Abel and learn all he could tell them about the matter. This he did, and the messengers obtained from Bishop Daniel a copy of the alphabet in question (which is said to have resembled the Greek) and information regarding the pronunciation of the letters composing it. Meanwhile the whole council, according to Lazarus Pharpetsi, addressed a very earnest request to the Katholicos that he would complete the work begun by his great ancestor Gregory, by taking immediate steps to have the Bible translated into Armenian from the Greek. Saḥak most gladly undertook to have this great work carried out, for he saw that it was the desire of the whole nation, who deeply felt their need and the almost utter uselessness of having the Scriptures read and divine service held in a language they could not understand.

A fitter person than Saḥak to undertake such a work could hardly have been found. Setting aside his piety and zeal, Saḥak's learning rendered him capable of the task. Born at Constantinople and educated there and at Caesarea, Saḥak knew Greek as perfectly as he knew his mother tongue. He had become Katholicos at the age of thirty-five, and the greater part of his life up to that time had been spent abroad. He had a very fair knowledge of Syriac, and was also well acquainted with Persian, at that time apparently the court language in Armenia. His energy was unbounded, and he *was* untiring in every good work. He commanded the confidence of the people and was honoured at court. Besides all this, he was an eloquent preacher and an able teacher, and had the rare talent of instilling into the minds of his disciples the zeal and earnestness that animated his own soul.

When Mesṛop received the alphabet sent by Bishop Daniel, Saḥak and he, having carefully studied it, tried for two whole years to teach it in the schools and use it for the development of an Armenian literature. But they found that it contained *fourteen letters less* than were actually needed to express the sounds of their native tongue. Mesṛop had devoted a considerable amount of study to the phonology of Armenian, and he came to the conclusion that it was utter waste of time to continue to use this defective alphabet. Before, however, abandoning the attempt, he, with his assistants John of Ekeghikh and Joseph Paghnatsi, visited Bishop Daniel in Mesopotamia, and tried with his assistance to modify this alphabet so as to adapt it to the Armenian language. But the attempt failed.

While praying over the matter the right solution suddenly occurred to Mesṛop. Koṛiun informs us that, 'Not in sleep as a dream, nor in a vision while awake, but in the workshop of his heart he saw, manifested to the eyes of his spirit, the fingers of a right hand writing on a rock. The stone had a border-line as of snow. It not only was manifested to him, but the exact figures of all the characters were collected together in his mind as if in a vase. Rising from prayer, he created our written characters. At Samosata he and his assistants procured the aid of a Greek scribe named Ruffinus, a disciple of Epiphanês, a hermit in Samos, who seems to have assisted him in improving and arranging the characters as far as possible in accordance with the order of the letters of the Greek alphabet. In fact, there can be no reasonable doubt that the Armenian characters are formed principally from the Greek, though some were apparently borrowed from the Avestic alphabet, and new letters—modifications of somewhat similar Greek ones—were introduced when needed to express sounds peculiar to Armenian. The alphabet thus formed was made symmetrical and harmonious, and it has ever since been used in Armenia. The date which Armenian historians assign for this invention is a.d. 406.

Immediately after this discovery, Mesṛop with his two pupils, John and Joseph, set to work to translate the Bible from the Greek. He began with the Book of Proverbs, and then went on to translate the New Testament. How much of this work he accomplished at Samosata we do not know. Koṛiun seems to imply that Mesṛop translated the whole Bible, while Moses of Khoṛenê attributes the work to him and the Katholicos Saḥak and their disciples working together. It seems plain that the whole task cannot have been accomplished by Mesṛop at that time for he returned to Armenia very soon, and we find the new invention warmly welcomed by King Vramshapouḥ's in 408, when he encouraged Mesṛop and Saḥak in their efforts to establish schools throughout the country, in which the new letters were taught. The school established at Vagharṣhapat was the most celebrated of these, and became in fact a sort of *Alma Mater* to all the rest. The pupils there trained were dispersed throughout the country to found schools and train the most promising youths in the other cantons of Armenia. They were also associated with Saḥak and Mesṛop in their translational work. Then began the Golden Age of Armenian literature. The fifth century is known as the Age of Translators. These were divided into two groups. Among the ' elder translators ' are included Eznik Koghbatsi, who wrote a refutation of heresies, Koṛiun the biographer of Mesṛop, Joseph Paghnatsi and John Ekeghetsatsi, whom we have already mentioned, Joseph Vayots Tzorits and Leontius Vanandetsi. The ' younger translators ' were in most instances the pupils of the elder, and included Moses of Khoṛenê (the Herodotus of Armenian history), Eghishê (Elisha), who wrote a history of the great struggle which took place in the fifth century between the Persians and the Armenians under the Vaṛdans, John Mandakouni, Ghazaṛ (Lazarus) Phaṛpetsi the historian, and others.

When Mesṛop returned to Armenia he found that the Katholicos had already begun to translate the Bible from the Syriac. It had been his intention to make the Greek Septuagint the basis of his translation of the Old Testament and to translate the New Testament from the original Greek. But a most careful search throughout the whole of Persian Armenia failed to discover a single manuscript of the Holy Scriptures in Greek. Meṛouzhan's search for Greek books had been so thorough that he had burned every single copy in the country. Nor were the Katholicos' messengers permitted to extend their search to that part of the country which, after *Khosṛov* Ill's death, had again, in the reign of

Theodosius II, been incorporated with the Byzantine empire. Even Mesṛop's attempts to get permission to teach his alphabet to the people of that district were for some considerable time successfully opposed by the Byzantine governors. Meṛouzhan's efforts had not been directed to the destruction of Syriac copies of the Bible ; in fact, Syriac learning was encouraged by the Persians, while they sternly endeavoured to repress the study of Greek. Hence Saḥak had no difficulty in procuring copies of the Peshiṭṭâ version of the Bible, and accordingly began to translate that into Armenian. He first translated those portions of the Scriptures which were appointed to be read in the churches, and his version of these was published in a.d. 411.

The Katholicos now sent some of his own and Mesṛop's most promising pupils to Greece and Syria to search for and translate all the most important books they could find, especially the works of the leading Fathers of the Church. Eznik and Joseph were sent to Edessa for this purpose. When they had made many versions there from the Syriac, they went to Constantinople in their eagerness to prosecute the study of Greek. There obtaining pos-session of the Greek originals of some of the works they already had in Syriac, they carefully revised the versions of these books which they had made at Edessa. They were joined at Constantinople by Koṛiun and Leontês, who had been impelled to go thither by their zeal for learning. Shortly afterwards two others of their fellow-students arrived, John and Aṛtzan, sent by Saḥak to obtain authorized copies of the Greek Bible for him, and these latter were also directed to be present at the Council of Ephesus in a.d. 431. There they gave an account of the progress of the Gospel in Armenia and of Mesṛop's great invention. On their return they took back with them copies of the Greek Bible from the imperial library at Constantinople, which must have been in accordance with those made by Eusebius at Constantine the Great's command. They found Mesṛop and Saḥak at Ashtishat, still busily engaged in translational work. On the receipt of the Greek MSS. which his messengers had brought, Saḥak was greatly puzzled by the numerous slight variations of reading to be found in the different Syriac and Greek copies of the Bible now in his hands. It was partly for this reason, as well as with the object of securing the assistance of scholars thoroughly versed in Greek learning, that he sent Moses of Khoṛenê and others to study philosophy, history and rhetoric at Alexandria. Others were sent to Constantinople and to other great educational centres. On their return, after a period of about seven years, these men devoted their energies to the enlightenment of their native land.

They do not seem, however, to have been of much assistance in the translation of the Bible, which was finished and published in a.d. 436. This was the *second* Armenian version, made this time by Saḥak and Mesṛop from the *Greek*. The receipt of the Greek MSS. brought from Byzantium had made Saḥak resolve to revise his version in accordance with the Greek. We might therefore suppose that he would have followed the Greek in all places where it differs from the Peshiṭṭâ Syriac text. But—however the fact is to be accounted for—this is by no means the case. Certain passages show that the Syriac text was preferred to the Greek. It will be sufficient to mention one illustration of this. In the last paragraph of St. Matthew's Gospel—which is read in the Baptismal Service of the Armenian Church—the passage, £As [My] Father hath sent Me, even so send I you,' is introduced at the end of the eighteenth verse, as in the Peshiṭṭâ. It is repeated, however, in the Armenian version (as in the Greek text and the Peshiṭṭâ) in its proper place, John xx. 21. Making allowances for such facts as these, which show a want of critical acumen—hardly to be wondered at in that age—on the part of the Armenian translators, the version made by Saḥak, Mesṛop and their coadjutors is a noble one, well deserving of the title of ' Queen of Versions,' which has been bestowed upon it. Its great defect is that the Old Testament was translated from the Septuagint, and not direct from the original Hebrew.

From the language of Moses of Khoṛenê and other contemporary writers, it is clear that the Armenian Bible did not originally contain the Apocrypha. The expression they use is that the translators rendered into Armenian the 'Twenty-two Evident (= Acknowledged) Books ' of the Old Testament. This of course means the books of the Hebrew canon, which were in ancient times reckoned as numbering twenty-two, the number of the letters in the Hebrew alphabet. The Old Testament Apocrypha is, however, now read in the Armenian Church.

As far as we can learn from the somewhat varying accounts of contemporary Armenian historians, the whole of the Old Testament, except the Proverbs of Solomon, was translated by Saḥak, while Mesṛop translated the Proverbs and the New Testament. But the revision was shared in by both these great men as well as some of the most able of their disciples. It is needless to say what a boon to Armenia such a work was. The Armenian people were now able to understand the Word of God read in their churches and circulated among them in every part of the country as quickly as scribes could multiply copies in sufficient numbers. The Bible was everywhere eagerly studied, and one immediate result was a great deepening of the religious life of the people. The knowledge of the Gospel message and of the commandments of God spread everywhere, and Mesṛop and Saḥak were most diligent in the effort to enlighten the people in every canton of the country. We may form some idea of what then took place in Armenia by remembering the accounts which historians give us of the reception Luther's German Bible met with when it issued from the press. The Armenian Bible soon became the one great national book, and early Armenian historians have in most cases their whole style coloured by their intimate acquaintance with Holy Scripture. It has often been remarked, and with perfect truth, that it was to the invention of the Armenian alphabet and the publication of Mesṛop and Saḥak's version of the Bible in that language that the nation owed not only its retention of Chris-tianity during the terrible persecution that so quickly followed the fall of the Arsacide dynasty, but even its very existence. Had not the people been united by an intelligent knowledge and a hearty acceptance of one faith, and by the possession of a national literature, they could never have weathered the storms that in the fifth and following centuries beat with such fury upon Armenia. The breathing-space afforded by Vramshapouḥ's wise and peaceful reign, falling between two periods of trouble and discord, was given by an All-wise and Merciful Providence to prevent the vessel of both Church and nationality from dire and terrible shipwreck.

Besides the direct spiritual results of the translation of the Bible into the language of the people (which were so great that Lazarus Pharpetsi says that in describing them he is warranted in using Isaiah's words, and stating that the whole land of Armenia was thereby 'filled with the knowledge of the Lord as the waters cover the sea '), it had also others less direct, but very important. One of these was that it reduced the language to a literary standard, and gave it order, fixity and permanence. From very early times many different dialects had prevailed in Armenia, but during the last few centuries of our narrative the dialect of the province of Ararat had come to the fore as the language of the court and of the central and leading district in the kingdom. This was the dialect which was naturally adopted by the translators, and it became the literary language of the country. Even to the present time, though no longer spoken, it is used in literature to a great extent, and until very recently was the only written form of Armenian. Two literary dialects of the modern language, those of Ararat and Constantinople, are now extensively used, though the old literary dialect is still dignified with the title of Gṛabaṛ, or 'written.'

The literary impulse given to the leading minds of the nation by Mesṛop's invention of the alphabet led to a great amount of other translational work, besides the composition of such books as Moses of *Khoṛenê's History of Armenia,* Eznik's *Refutation of Heresies,* Elisha's *History of the War of the Vaṛdans,* and other similar works of great value and interest. Not only were the old chronicles of the kingdom transcribed into the new alphabet, and thus preserved for some considerable time, but the works of all the Greek and Syrian Fathers that could possibly be obtained were translated into Armenian. A little later the works of Plato and Aristotle, of Homer and other classical writers, were added to the list. We hardly know as yet at all fully what valuable writings have thus been preserved to us in Armenian libraries, but Tatian's *Diatessaron* and Eusebius' *Chronicle* are examples of the treasures still to be discovered by diligent search in this field of learning.

Armenian historians relate that to Mesṛop is due the invention of the ecclesiastical alphabet in use in Georgia. The date they fix for this is a.d. 410. But the Georgians deny the fact ; and the circumstance that those Georgian letters which in form bear a resemblance to certain letters of the Armenian alphabet have an entirely different value, renders it very questionable. It is also said that in a.d. 423 he drew up an alphabet for the Alvanians, who spoke a dialect of Armenian, in order to enable their Archbishop Jeremiah to translate the Bible into that language for his people's use. This version, however, is no longer extant.

Thus was finished the work which had been begun perhaps as early as the days of the apostles, and had been mightily revived by Gregory the Illuminator. Armenia was now a Christian country, with an independent and indigenous Church, and a Bible in her own language. She possessed a body of devout and learned clergy, full of energy and zeal. Her students went everywhere to seek knowledge and learning, and returned home to divide among her numerous congregations the mental and spiritual treasures they had won. Her people studied the Word of God, and grew in grace and in the knowledge of God. Christianity had routed and annihilated paganism, and had struck her roots deep down into the heart and conscience of the nation. Like a noble tree on the mountain-top, buffeted by the storm and yet unshaken from its post, the Armenian Church, even in the near future, was to experience the tempests of persecution and oppression, and yet by those very blasts be driven to strike root more deeply still, as it were, into the very Rock of Ages, and to stand firm during all future time as a proof of her Masters protecting care in the very face of the gates of hell.

CHAPTER XIV

CONCLUSION

We have now reached the conclusion of our task. We have hastily glanced at the history of the Armenian nation from the earliest times to the birth of our Lord. We have learned something about the geography and the ancient mythology of the land, have noticed the leading characteristics of the people, and have briefly sketched the political changes that occurred up to the fall of the Arsacide dynasty. The account of the first introduction of Christianity into the country has naturally led us to undertake a fuller study of the life and times of St. Gregory the Illumi-nator, the Apostle of Armenia. We have seen how many noble men and women were called upon to lay down their lives for the faith ere Armenia was finally won for Christ. We have learnt how earnestly many of Gregory's own descendants toiled and suffered for the spread of the Gospel, and how ultimately, during the patriarchate, and largely through the personal efforts of the last of Gregory's line who held that high office, the whole Bible was given to the people in their copious and eloquent mother-tongue, and by them accepted and prized as the very food of their souls. Our duty was to detail the history of the conversion of Armenia to the Christian faith. It does not fall to our lot, therefore, to relate the long and tragic tale of the later history of the Armenian Church and nation, or to tell how often and how nobly (as during even the last few years) Armenians have shed their blood for their Saviour. Few countries in the world can show so long and so noble a martyrology —one, alas ! not yet closed.

It does not lie within our province to discuss the present state of the venerable Armenian Church. It would be an ungracious task in citizens of a more favoured nation to cast a stone at a Church that has suffered, and still suffers, so much oppression and wrong from the enemies of our common faith. May we not rather trust and pray that the light which God so long ago kindled in Armenia may not be permitted to be extinguished by Muslim cruelty and intolerance at the close of this nineteenth Christian century ? Nay, rather may it be revived by the gracious influences of the Holy Spirit, and shine more clearly than ever before ! May the leaders of that Church in our own day and generation be roused to hear even now—as the noble Saḥak did in the beginning of the fifth century—the sighs of multitudes of her people, who now as then go forth from their churches (to use Lazarus Phaṛpetsi's words) empty in spirit and uncomforted, because of the use of a dead language which they cannot understand, but in which they are compelled to worship God. May they follow the example of Saḥak and Mesṛop, and restore to the people in their beloved mother-tongue the living oracles of God ! Then we may hope that Armenian faith and zeal will once more burn brightly, and that our Armenian brethren may be enabled to repay to the benighted land of Persia the debt which they owe to the fatherland of Gregory and Saḥak the Parthian, by handing on to the Muslims of that land the torch of Divine Truth which those patriarchs kindled in Armenia in days of yore.

The present century has witnessed the resurrection of more than one ancient nation. Greece and Italy have risen, like the fabled Phoenix, from their ashes, and are striving to emulate the glories of their past history. We, who see signs of the coming restoration of the kingdom to Israel, may well hope that, in some way known only to the All-Wise Lord of all, the early years of the twentieth century may see Armenia too, Israel's rival in suffering, rising to a new and glorious life, and sharing in the great work of preparing the way of our returning Lord. We believe that all things, in this God's world, work together for good, and we

'Trust that somehow good
Will be the final goal of ill,

That nothing walks with aimless feet ;
That not one life shall be destroyed,
Or cast as rubbish to the void,
When God hath made the pile complete.'

And we cannot but feel confident that God, who has led His Armenian Church for so many ages in the wilderness of affliction, will at last lead her to the land of promise, and grant her and her children in the Master's presence the rest that remaineth for the people of God.

APPENDIX

A great deal has been written upon the ' Abgar Legend,' as it has been called ; and the general opinion of European men of learning is decidedly opposed to its acceptance as embodying any historical fact. But it seems to the writer that scepticism in this matter, as in all others, has its limits. The fact that both Eusebius and Moses of *Khoṛenê* assure us that they derived their statements on the subject from ancient Syriac documents still preserved in their days in the royal library of Edessa, which city both authors had themselves visited, seems of itself sufficient to make us consider whether it is certain that such documents were merely clumsy and recent forgeries, or whether they may not have been documents regarded—and rightly so—even then as ancient and of great importance. Briefly, what other information we have on the subject is as follows :—

In Armenian there exist two certainly very ancient compositions, entitled respectively *Abgar's Letter to Christ* and the *Martyrology of St. Thaddaeus the Apostle.* The Armenian version of these documents was made early in the fifth century, and was evidently taken from a Syriac original. Moses of Khoṛenê, writing comparatively early in that century (his *His-tory* ends in A. d. 440), states that he had used as his authority for the facts he relates about Sanatṛouk and the martyrdom of Thaddaeus and Sandoukht the annals written at the time by the contemporary court scribe, whose name, in the edition of Moses of Khoṛenê which I am quoting (printed at Amsterdam in 1692), is written ' *Gheṛoubnah,* son of Aphshadaṛ the scribe' *(Patm. Ḥayots,* Hat. ii, kl. 33), who, he says, 'wrote all the deeds which were done in the days of Abgar and Sanatṛouk, and placed the book in the library at Edessa.' Some old MSS. of this work of Gheṛoubnah (or, as others read the name, Laboubnia or Laboubnia—the *Gh* in Armenian being almost optionally interchangeable with *L,* and the letters for *b* and *r* being almost undistinguishable) have been discovered and published during the last thirty years. The author of the able works on ancient Armenian literature, entitled *Ḥaikakan Ḥin Dpṛouthian Patmouthiun* and *Matenadaṛan Ḥaikakan Thaṛgmanoutheants Nakhneats* (Venice, 1886 and 1889 respectively), gives good reason for concluding (1) that the Armenian text of these MSS. is really that of the old Armenian version made in the fifth century from the Syriac, and (2) that the original Syriac text was written by a contemporary of Abgar and Sanatṛouk. The Armenian MSS. entirely *disprove* the genuineness of the supposed letter of Christ to Abgar, which has long been perceived to bear the marks of being in some way or other spurious. Instead of saying (as Moses of *Khoṛenê* does) that our Lord dictated to Thomas His reply to Abgar's letter, Laboubnia writes thus : ' Jesus, having received the letter ' (from Abgar's envoy) ' in the house of the high priest of the Jews, saith to Anan, the king's confidant, " Go thou, say to thy lord who sent thee unto Me, Blessed art thou, because thou hast believed in Me without having yet seen Me, for so is it written concerning Me," &c. The message was a *verbal* one, according to Laboubnia. We can easily see how the words of the message were afterwards mistaken for an actual letter written at our Lord's dictation. The story of the portrait of Christ which was brought to Abgar is also very simply narrated by the author of the document in question in these words : ' [Anan] took and painted a picture of Jesus with rare colours, for he was the king's artist, and he brought and gave it over to King Abgar his lord.' The letter of Abgar to Christ as given by Laboubnia is almost identical with that quoted by Eusebius and Moses of Khoṛenê, almost the only difference being that, while at the beginning of the letter Eusebius and Moses of Khoṛenê represent the king as giving Christ the title of ' the Good *Saviour!* or ' the Beneficent *Saviour'* Laboubnia has instead the words 'the Great *Physician' (bzhishk* instead of *phṛkichh),* which were certainly much more likely to be used by Abgar in writing such a letter to seek for healing.

More light has been thrown on the subject of the truth or otherwise of the narrative by Cureton's discovery in 1848 of portions of two Syriac MSS., containing the original documents from which the Armenian versions were made in the fifth century. Dr. Wright believes that one of these MSS. was written at the beginning of that century, and the other in the sixth century. He published them in 1864 with the title, *Ancient Syriac Documents relative to the earliest establishment of Christianity in Edessa.* As far as these go, they agree very well with the Armenian version, the only difference of much importance being that, after Thaddaeus' visit to Edessa, the Armenian version represents him as journeying thence towards the East, while the Syriac merely relates his death.

It remains only to add that, at the end of one of the Armenian MSS. of the translation into that language of the *Martyrology of Thaddaeus,* the translator has written as follows : ' I, Bishop Samuel, an unworthy servant of Christ, have translated the *Martyrology* of the holy apostle Thaddaeus and of the holy virgin Sandoukht, and have given it to the whole land of Armenia.' Moses of Khoṛenê speaks of the whole narrative of Sandoukht's martyrdom and that of Thaddaeus as having been written by others before his time, and as already well known in Armenia, *and hence he* repeats it only very briefly. The document to which he refers was most probably this version of Bishop Samuel's . The author of *Ḥaikakan Thaṛgmanouthiunkh* believes that both Laboubnia's work and this *Martyrology* (a continuation of the former, but probably by a different hand), though having apparently in the course of time undergone a certain amount of corruption, interpolation and perhaps other alterations, bear upon them the undoubted marks of antiquity. On the whole it seems to the present writer that, though it would be rash to assert the genuineness of Abgar's letter to Christ or the fact of his baptism, yet there can be little doubt that Christianity was introduced as early as the first century into Armenia, and that many of those who first accepted it there, as elsewhere, were called upon to seal their testimony with their blood.

Made in the USA
Columbia, SC
07 December 2021

50657315R00035